T0305923

Artificial Intelligence in Accounting

Artificial Intelligence in Accounting: Practical Applications was written with a simple goal — to provide accountants with a foundational understanding of AI and its many business and accounting applications. It is meant to serve as a guide for identifying opportunities to implement AI initiatives to increase productivity and profitability.

This book will help you answer questions about what AI is and how it is used in the contemporary accounting profession. By offering practical guidance that can further benefit your practice or organization, this book provides an overview of essential AI concepts and technologies that accountants should know such as machine learning, deep learning, and natural language processing. It also describes accounting-specific applications of robotic process automation and text mining. Illustrated with case studies and interviews with representatives from global professional services firms, this concise volume makes a significant contribution to examining the intersection of AI and the accounting profession.

This innovative book also explores the challenges and ethical considerations of AI. It will be of great interest and benefit to accounting practitioners, researchers, educators, and students.

Cory Ng is an Associate Professor of Instruction in Accounting at the Fox School of Business at Temple University in Philadelphia, Pennsylvania, USA.

John Alarcon is the founder of BEARN, a business advisory firm in Philadelphia, Pennsylvania, USA.

Routledge Focus on Business and Management

The fields of business and management have grown exponentially as areas of research and education. This growth presents challenges for readers trying to keep up with the latest important insights. Routledge Focus on Business and Management presents small books on big topics and how they intersect with the world of business research.

Individually, each title in the series provides coverage of a key academic topic, whilst collectively, the series forms a comprehensive collection across the business disciplines.

Entrepreneurial Urban Regeneration
Business Improvement Districts as a Form of Organizational Innovation
Rezart Prifti and Fatma Jaupi

Strategic University Management
Future Proofing Your Institution
Loren Falkenberg and M. Elizabeth Cannon

Innovation in Africa
Fuelling an Entrepreneurial Ecosystem for Growth and Prosperity
Deseye Umurhohwo

Consumer Behaviour and Social Network Sites
The Impact of Negative Word of Mouth
Sarah Zaraket

Artificial Intelligence in Accounting
Practical Applications
Cory Ng and John Alarcon

Digitalised Talent Management
Navigating the Human-Technology Interface
Edited by Sharna Wiblen

For more information about this series, please visit: www.routledge.com/ Routledge-Focus-on-Business-and-Management/book-series/FBM

Artificial Intelligence in Accounting
Practical Applications

Cory Ng and John Alarcon

Routledge
Taylor & Francis Group

NEW YORK AND LONDON

First published 2021
by Routledge
52 Vanderbilt Avenue, New York, NY 10017

and by Routledge
2 Park Square, Milton Park, Abingdon, Oxon, OX14 4RN

*Routledge is an imprint of the Taylor & Francis Group, an
informa business*

Library of Congress Cataloging-in-Publication Data

Names: Ng, Cory, 1975- author. | Alarcon, John, 1964- author.
Title: Artificial intelligence in accounting : practical applications /
Cory Ng and John Alarcon.
Description: New York, NY : Routledge, 2021. | Series: Routledge focus on
business and management | Includes bibliographical references and index.
Identifiers: LCCN 2020037635 (print) | LCCN 2020037636 (ebook) | ISBN
9780367431778 (hardback) | ISBN 9781003003342 (ebook)
Subjects: LCSH: Accounting--Technological innovations. | Artificial
intelligence.
Classification: LCC HF5636 .N42 2021 (print) | LCC HF5636 (ebook) | DDC
657.0285/63--dc23
LC record available at https://lccn.loc.gov/2020037635
LC ebook record available at https://lccn.loc.gov/2020037636

ISBN: 978-0-367-43177-8 (hbk)
ISBN: 978-1-003-00334-2 (ebk)

Typeset in Times New Roman
by MPS Limited, Dehradun

Contents

List of Illustrations

Foreword

Lately, much has been written about the change in pace and transformation of the accounting profession. This change is accelerating at an exponential rate, and CPAs and accountants are racing to meet the evolving demands of their clients and businesses. Often referred to as the Fourth Industrial Revolution, this digital explosion is being fueled by emerging and evolving technologies.

It is my pleasure to introduce you to *Artificial Intelligence in Accounting: Practical Applications* by Cory Ng, CPA, DBA, CGMA, and John Alarcon, CPA, DBA, CGMA. I am acquainted with both Cory and John as longtime authors and editorial board members for the *Pennsylvania CPA Journal*, the flagship publication of the Pennsylvania Institute of Certified Public Accountants (PICPA), and have long been impressed with their ability to clearly articulate complex issues to PICPA's 20,000 members.

Cory and John have a wealth of experience that makes them eminently qualified to discuss artificial intelligence. After developing a career in both public and private accounting, Cory is now an associate professor of instruction and the undergraduate program coordinator in the Department of Accounting at the Fox School of Business at Temple University. In addition to his work for the PICPA, including being a member of our Board of Directors, Cory has taught courses in data analytics, enterprise systems, information technology controls, and data visualization. John is the owner and principal of BEARN, a corporate finance and risk advisory firm in Philadelphia, and has served as an adjunct instructor at the Fox School of Business. John has over 25 years of experience serving in executive roles in both public and private companies.

The accounting profession has long been associated with continuous learning. This learning, however, is not only driven by evolving standards and laws but also by the nonstop application of technological innovation. Accountants view technology as an opportunity rather than a threat. Tools like artificial intelligence, robotic process automation, blockchain, and machine learning – and the requisite skills to apply them – provide a competitive edge for accountants and elevate their position as trusted business advisers.

According to the most recent (2018) World Economic Forum *Future of Jobs* report, current employees will need over 100 days of retraining and upskilling over the next two years. In addition to technical competency, other skills that will grow in prominence include analytical thinking, innovation, and active learning strategies. Understanding the capabilities and increasing the use of tools such as artificial intelligence will provide accountants with a path forward to grow their skills.

Development growth in technology has and continues to impact lives, and some wonder whether all this new technology will displace accountants. I actually believe the opposite – accountants are moving forward. The profession acknowledges the need for upskilling, not only for those currently in the workforce but also for the skills being taught in accounting programs in colleges and universities. Incorporating new skills into the learning track for the profession helps the industry attract the best and brightest students and provide them with the tools they need to become trusted business advisers.

Learning and implementing technology to improve processes is not an option but a business imperative. Companies that survive and thrive during the Fourth Industrial Revolution will be those that embrace the opportunities that new technology provides. Many will rely upon their accountants to initiate the conversion to understand and use the most current technology tools available to ensure innovation and success.

All participants in the accounting profession need to be well-equipped with the skills to meet the ever-changing demands of their clients and companies. Cory and John are doing their part to create more highly-skilled, digitally proficient talent by providing practical applications for artificial intelligence. What differentiates this book from many of the others written on using AI in business, is that it is specific to the unique needs of the accounting profession. I strongly encourage accountants and students to embrace the opportunities these tools afford and to use them to elevate the status of the accounting profession.

Michael D. Colgan, CAE, CEO & Executive Director,
Pennsylvania Institute of Certified Public Accountants

Preface

Artificial intelligence (AI) is embedded in our everyday lives – think of the predictive technology used by Amazon or Netflix that provides personalized recommendations based on past viewing or purchasing behavior. Companies use AI-enabled technology to improve business processes and generate better insights. Yet, we are still in the early days of AI adoption. Business leaders' potential to leverage AI to gain a competitive advantage is enormous, especially for those in the accounting profession who are charged with measuring economic activity and communicating that information to decision-makers.

Artificial Intelligence in Accounting: Practical Applications was written with a simple goal – to provide accountants with a foundational understanding of AI and its many business and accounting applications. It is meant to serve as a guide for identifying opportunities to implement AI initiatives to increase productivity and profitability.

This book will help you answer questions about what AI is and how it is being used in the accounting profession today. Offering practical guidance that you can apply to your organization, we provide an overview of AI concepts that accountants should know, followed by detailed examples of AI applications currently used in practice. Next, we examine accounting-specific applications of robotic process automation and text mining, two important domains where AI innovation promises to have particularly profound transformative effects on the profession in the coming years. We also share valuable lessons from in-depth interviews conducted with AI technology leaders from KPMG LLP, Ernst & Young LLP, Deloitte & Touche LLP, and Grant Thornton LLP. The promise of AI is not without risk - we balance the potential benefits of AI with a discussion of the challenges and ethical considerations of AI implementations. Finally, we conclude by speculating on the future outlook for the accounting profession and AI.

In recognizing the important role that AI-enabled technology will play in the years to come, we hope that this book will be a valuable resource for practicing accountants and educators in preparing students to enter the profession.

Acknowledgments

We would like to thank Temple University, the Fox School of Business Office of the Dean, and the Department of Accounting for their support of this project. We are grateful for the following individuals, who served as reviewers for this book: Matthew MacNaughton from the Office of Research & Doctoral Programs of the Fox School of Business; Randy Johnston of Network Management Group, Inc. and K2 Enterprises; and Doug Listman of Cohen & Company. We would also like to recognize the contributions of Temple University student Rose Listman. In addition, we are thankful for the following individuals for their contributions: Mike Colgan of the Pennsylvania Institute of Certified Public Accountants; Steve Hill, Vinodh Swaminathan, Komal Dhall, and Thomas Herr of KPMG LLP; Jennifer Samuel of KPMG International; Sean Seymour of Ernst & Young LLP; Brian Crowley of Deloitte & Touche LLP; and Christopher Spratt of Grant Thornton LLP.

Finally, and most importantly, we remain thankful for the support and encouragement of our families: Rashida, Asia, and Caleb Ng; Cynthia Ng; Charlie and Tommi Ng; Edward and Helen Moseé; John Street; Andrea Krupp, Thomas, Mathilde, and Clement Alarcon, and other members of the Alarcon family.

1 What Accountants Need to Know

Introduction

Artificial Intelligence (AI) is transforming how we live and work. Intelligent virtual assistants on smartphones (e.g., Siri on Apple devices), facial recognition software on social media platforms (e.g., Facebook), and self-driving autonomous vehicles (e.g., Tesla) all utilize AI. Hospitals used AI in the battle against Covid-19. For example, Tampa General Hospital in Florida has deployed an AI system that performs facial thermal scans on patients entering the building to detect potential coronavirus symptoms such as sweat, discoloration, and fever (Wittbold et al., 2020). The convergence of big data analytics, advances in computing power, the Internet of Things (IoT), and large scale investment by governments, universities, and high-tech organizations such as Google, Amazon, Microsoft, and IBM have accelerated the adoption of AI for consumers and businesses.

These cases are just a few examples of the digital transformation we are currently experiencing, an era described by Klaus Schwab, founder and executive chairman of the World Economic Forum, as "The Fourth Industrial Revolution". Schwab notes that the current revolution is distinct from the previous three due to the velocity of technological change, the breadth and depth of these technologies, and its impact on entire systems (i.e., countries, companies, industries, and society as a whole) (Schwab, 2017). AI is one of the key technologies driving this digital revolution.

So, what exactly is AI? **Artificial intelligence** is a computer program or software application that can imitate or simulate human behavior. AI applications are expected to automate a significant portion of the repetitive tasks performed by accountants, though the implications of this change for the accounting profession has divided scholars. Some critics speculate that sufficiently sophisticated AI will eliminate the need for accountants in the future. Others predict that the accounting profession will experience increased productivity and cost savings by incorporating AI technology. What is evident on both sides is that AI will have a significant impact on the accounting profession in the coming decades. As we will discuss throughout this book, and in more detail in Chapter 7, our view is that AI will not eliminate the need for accountants but empower them to deliver more accurate, timely, and forward-looking insights into the business(es). As part of the impending transformation of the profession, accountants will need to develop the skills necessary to provide mission-critical judgment and oversight of AI-enabled systems and processes in order for organizations to realize productivity gains and meet other objectives expected from AI. The purpose of this book is to provide accountants with a practical guide for identifying opportunities to implement artificial intelligence (AI) initiatives to increase productivity and profitability.

History of AI

Given the recent widespread media coverage on AI, the field of AI may seem like a new discipline. However, the roots of AI's can be traced back to 1943 when neurophysiologist Warren McCulloch and logic expert Walter Pitts proposed the first model of artificial neurons (Russell & Norvig, 2010). The field of AI was established as an academic and research discipline when the first AI conference was organized at Dartmouth College in 1956 (Bringsjord & Govindarajulu, 2018). Today, AI is an interdisciplinary field of science, engineering, statistics, philosophy, neuroscience, psychology, computer engineering, and others.

History of Accountants Using Technology

Technology has always played an important role in accounting for business transactions through the ages – from the use of an abacus over 2,000 years ago (New York State Society of CPAs, 2015), to the purchase of a computer in 1955 exclusively for accounting purposes (Untapped Editorial Team, 2018), to the creation of electronic spreadsheets in the 1980s (Pepe, 2011). AI is the next significant technological advancement that will play an essential role in the accounting profession for years to come.

Overview of How Accountants Are Using AI

Accountants currently use AI in a variety of applications, from identifying high-risk transactions in audits to performing accounts payable processing tasks. As a result, AI is increasingly taking the place of human processing and decision-making, which will continue to have a transformative impact on business practices. Although AI adoption in the accounting profession is in its early stages, practitioners must understand the implications of this technology.

The adoption of AI has been on a steady rise in both public and corporate accounting. For example, EY[1] uses AI drones to perform inventory counts with increased accuracy and efficiency. Deloitte[2] uses a tool called "Argus" to extract critical accounting information from any type of electronic document to improve the quality and efficiency of an audit (Deloitte, 2015). In management accounting, AI is used to automatically code accounting entries, forecast revenues, and analyze unstructured data such as contracts and emails (ICAEW, 2017).

Going forward, it is even more exciting to think about how AI will be used in accounting. Imagine if you could ask an intelligent virtual assistant (such as Alexa or Siri) to analyze accounts payable for duplicate payments as part of your audit procedures. Technological advances in artificial intelligence could make this possible very soon. Researchers Burns and Igou (2019) suggest that accountants should consider using intelligent virtual assistants to interface with AI applications to perform audit analysis, data retrieval, spreadsheet creation, and data visualizations – all activated by human commands.

Human Intelligence versus Artificial Intelligence

For more than 2,000 years, philosophers have pondered questions such as "how does the human mind work?" and "can non-humans have minds?" (Negnevitsky, 2011, p. 1). The Merriam-Webster dictionary (2020) defines intelligence as follows:

1   The ability to learn or understand or to deal with new or trying situations
2   The ability to apply knowledge to manipulate one's environment or to abstractly think as measured by objective criteria (such as tests)

For decades, scholars in the field of psychology have debated what constitutes human intelligence (Weiner & Freedheim, 2013). Some experts describe human intelligence as the capacity for "reasoning, problem solving and learning" (Colom et al., 2010). Additional common characteristics of human intelligence include logical thinking, spatial perception, and pattern recognition (Yao et al., 2018). Human intelligence also involves the ability to perceive, understand, and predict (Russell & Norvig, 2010) as well as the capacity for planning and adaptability (Siegel et al., 2003).

The goal of AI is to build machines that "can perform complex tasks as well as, or better than, humans. In order to perform those complex tasks, machines must be able to perceive, reason, learn, and communicate" (Siegel et al., 2003, p. 1). Achieving this goal has been the quest of computer scientists and engineers for more than half a decade. Computers are very good at performing specific tasks, such as complex math calculations, with speed and accuracy. Yet, today's computers are not as good at performing tasks such as abstract reasoning, concept formulation, and strategic planning (Yao et al., 2018).

What Accountants Need to Know About AI

Artificial intelligence is divided into a variety of sub-fields, including but not limited to machine reasoning, machine learning, deep learning, and natural language processing. Each of these sub-fields has essential applications in accounting. In effect, AI has fields that may even be nested as sub-fields, such as Deep Learning (DL) is a sub-field of Machine Learning (ML), as illustrated in Figure 1.1.

Artificial Intelligence

As stated in the introduction, artificial intelligence is defined broadly as a computer program or software application that can imitate or simulate human behavior. This definition works well with a variety of technologies that we use every day. For example, the words that you are currently reading were spoken into a dictation tool in a popular word processing software. This form of AI uses speech recognition software to translate audio data into text, mimicking the actions of a human transcriber.

However, it is important to recognize that a generally accepted definition of artificial intelligence remains open for debate (Dobrev, 2012). An influential textbook in AI research entitled *Artificial Intelligence: A Modern Approach* offers four possibilities: systems that think like humans, systems that act like humans, systems that think rationally, and systems that act rationally (Russell & Norvig, 2010).

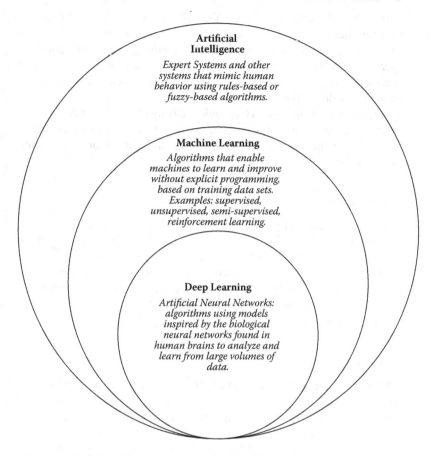

Figure 1.1 Relationship between AI, ML, and DL.

Today speech recognition is considered a form of AI and tomorrow it may be relegated to straightforward automation. The bottom line here is that what constitutes AI continues to evolve with time and technological advances. Although a consensus may not exist on a formal definition of AI, experts often make a distinction between two subtypes of AI – artificial narrow intelligence (ANI) and artificial general intelligence (AGI).

Artificial Narrow Intelligence (ANI)

Artificial narrow intelligence (ANI), also known as weak or narrow AI, focuses on a task, such as speech recognition, computers that can play chess, or autonomous vehicles. Virtually all of the AI with which we are familiar can be classified as ANI, as computer scientists have yet to create machines that can experience emotion and the ability to perceive or feel things (Jajal, 2018). ANI machines that are programmed for these specific tasks are typically much better than their humans at doing the same task.

Examples of narrow AI include chatbots that are built for the narrow purpose of conversation. Chatbots are capable of verbal responses, using algorithms and a database, based on a statement or question.

Artificial General Intelligence (AGI)

The goal of **artificial general intelligence (AGI)**, also known as strong or broad AI, is to create machines capable of performing all the cognitive tasks of the human brain. The essential elements of AGI include: (1) the ability to apply knowledge from one domain to another; (2) the ability to plan for the future based on experience and knowledge; and (3) the ability to adapt based on changing circumstances (Walch, 2019).

Machine Reasoning

Machine reasoning (MR) is the ability of a computer to draw conclusions from a knowledge base using automated inference techniques that can imitate or simulate human inference, such as deduction and induction. León Bottou, a reasoning expert, provides a more technical definition of MR as an "algebraic manipulation of previously acquired knowledge in order to answer a new question" (Bottou, 2014, p. 136).

Expert Systems

The initial applications of reasoning systems were referred to as expert systems (ES). **Expert systems** are an early form of AI, first developed in the 1970s. They are computer systems that store knowledge from human experts to emulate human decision-making. To become an expert, one must have deep knowledge of both facts and rules as well as practical experience in a particular domain (Negnevitsky, 2011). Such expertise can be gained through formal training or hands-on experience. ES works by making recommendations or drawing conclusions on a narrow topic using a rules-based engine applied against a database. ES is used in a variety of disciplines in accounting, such as audit, tax, management accounting, and personal financial planning (Yang & Vasarhelyi, 1993).

Expert systems can be classified as rules-based or fuzzy-based. Rules-based expert systems employ a set of detailed instructions, called **algorithms**, that apply rules to interpret how to react to various scenarios. For example, a tax software program may use the following rule: if the adjusted gross income equals X dollars, then the applicable federal tax is equal to Y dollars.

Fuzzy-based expert systems use fuzzy logic – a logical system in which conditions cannot be described in binary terms such as true or false, 0 or 1. Fuzzy logic is useful in situations that involve imprecision and vagueness (Negnevitsky, 2011). For example, an algorithm using fuzzy logic was used in an expert system designed to assist with fraud detection of settled insurance claims (Pathak et al., 2005). These researchers also suggest that fuzzy logic expert systems could be used by auditors to assess control risks and detection risks on an audit engagement.

Today's machine reasoning systems go beyond the rules-based capabilities of ES. AI-enabled MR systems can now learn using machine learning algorithms and artificial neural networks to draw conclusions through data analysis. As a result, there are vast opportunities for accountants to utilize MR systems to enhance productivity.

Machine Learning

Machine learning (ML) is a subset of AI (as illustrated in Figure 1.1) that uses algorithms to analyze data to carry out specific tasks, such as making predictions, without relying on explicit programming as in rule-based expert systems. Machine learning uses pattern recognition and inference to learn from data. The larger the data set, the more examples from which the algorithm can learn through trial and error (CPA Canada, & AICPA, 2019). Machine learning is used by Netflix to make recommendations for TV shows and movies based on what the user previously viewed, thereby enhancing the user experience. The more content that a machine learning AI views, the more refined and accurate its predictions will be. To cite another example, Amazon uses machine learning to analyze purchasing data on its products to forecast demand, identify fraudulent purchases, and provide customized recommendations and promotions (Camhi & Pandolh, 2017).

We have so far discussed machine learning in consumer-driven fields, but what does it have to offer the field of accounting?

Since machine learning enables systems to be adaptative (Negnevitsky, 2011), computers equipped with ML can learn from experience, resulting in improved performance over time. As an example, KPMG[3] employs IBM's machine learning algorithms to assist their clients with compliance with the IFRS 16 lease accounting standard (Samuel, 2018). Specifically, the KPMG Contract Abstraction Tool extracts data from tens of thousands of contracts, each of which may be hundreds of pages long, and analyzes the data for compliance with the leasing standard. As the program examines more contracts, it becomes "smarter" and can offer more refined and targeted feedback. Markus Kreher, Global Head of Accounting Advisory Services and Head of Finance Advisory, KPMG in Germany, said: "We've effectively trained the solution to read and understand contracts just like an attorney would" (Samuel, 2018, para. 4).

Similarly, Deloitte uses an award-winning machine learning tool called Argus to review, identify, and extract key accounting information from any type of electronic document. Argus learns from every human interaction and can analyze sales and leasing contracts, employment agreements, invoices, meeting minutes, financial statements, and legal letters (Deloitte, 2015), eliminating a time-consuming and costly manual task normally performed by auditors. Thus, Argus enables Deloitte auditors to be more productive by spending their time interpreting results and exercising professional skepticism.

Possible applications for ML in accounting include computers that learn from audit failures by analyzing data sets that were the basis for incorrectly issuing a clean audit opinion. Another application of ML could be on tax positions taken by firms that were rejected by the federal and state tax authorities.

There are four main types of machine learning: supervised, unsupervised, semi-supervised, and reinforced.

Supervised Learning

Supervised learning is a process in which a computer algorithm learns from a set of training data that is labeled (tagged with certain attributes such as poor credit or good credit) and paired as input and output variables (X results in Y). Supervised learning is often used for classification (e.g., identifying fraudulent and non-fraudulent transactions) and prediction (e.g., predicting the number of uncollectible accounts based on the aging of individual customers). For example, suppose an auditor wants to predict the number of uncollectible accounts based on the aging of customer balances.

A developer would provide the model with historical data that includes the input variable (aging of individual customers) and the output data (amount of uncollectible accounts written off). A supervised ML model would then "learn" the rules based on the historical data and then predict the amount of uncollectible accounts when new aging data is provided.

Unsupervised Learning

Unsupervised learning, on the other hand, is a process in which the computer algorithm only learns from unlabeled input data (i.e., the outputs are unknown). For example, consider a controller of an accounting department who wants to better understand why customers do not pay within 30 days. An unsupervised machine learning model would teach the algorithm to identify trends and patterns related to the input data. The algorithm might identify that customers with outstanding accounts receivable balances over 120 days might have similar zip codes, income levels, or credit scores. One of the most common approaches for unsupervised learning is cluster analysis, whereby input data is grouped based on similarities.

Semi-supervised Learning

Semi-supervised learning is a hybrid of supervised and unsupervised learning using both labeled and unlabeled data during the training process. As many real-world data sets often contain incorrect or missing labels (Yao et al., 2018), using a semi-supervised approach could lead to improved learning compared to a purely supervised or unsupervised method.

Reinforcement Learning

Reinforcement learning is a process in which a computer algorithm trains itself, learning from data through trial and error. The agent is rewarded for performing specific tasks correctly and penalized for performing tasks incorrectly. These algorithms are designed to maximize rewards and minimize penalties.

Deep Learning

Deep learning (DL) is a subset of machine learning (as illustrated in Figure 1.1) that uses artificial neural networks to discover patterns from data. **Artificial neural networks (ANNs)** are a collection of artificial neurons (also known as units) that receive data as an input, and then logic is applied to produce an output. ANNs are frequently used for pattern recognition such as facial recognition in pictures and videos, speech recognition, social networks, etc., frequently accelerated by tensor processing. A **tensor processing unit (TPU)** is an application-specific circuit developed by Google that is used to increase processing speeds for machine learning and deep learning applications. Whereas traditional machine learning relies heavily on the guidance provided by human programmers, DL models use ANNs (inspired by the biological neural networks found in human brains) to analyze large volumes of data to teach itself.

Deep learning can be used in a variety of applications, such as facial recognition, image classification, speech recognition, and text translation. Current applications of DL include self-driving vehicles that slow down as it approaches a pedestrian cross-walk, ATM machines that reject a counterfeit banknote, and a smartphone app that translates the image of a street sign in a foreign language (The Mathworks & MATLAB, 2018).

EY uses deep learning technology to reconstruct documents (e.g., invoices and contracts used during an audit) that were poorly-scanned using optical recognition software (Duffy, 2019). Researcher Sophia Sun (2019) promotes the use of DL to support audit decision making in two key areas: information identification and judgment support. DL algorithms can analyze semi-structured data (e.g., text data from supporting documents such as invoices, contracts, etc.) and unstructured data (such as images, audio, and video from the internet, social media, etc.), which will aid in information identification. Further, Sun notes that the predictive performance of DL models is superior to classic machine learning when the volume of data and the number of variables is large. To maximize the use of DL in an audit context, Sun suggests designing and developing a data warehouse to train the algorithms to make predictions and assist with audit procedures.

Natural Language Processing

Natural language processing (NLP) is a subfield of AI that focuses on the interaction of computers and people using human languages. The Siri application on Apple's iPhone and Amazon's Alexa uses NLP to understand requests for completing a task.

NLP can be broken down into two types: natural language understanding and natural language generation.

Natural language understanding (NLU) enables computers to understand instructions provided in human language. For example, when a user asks their iPhone for weather conditions by using the following voice command, "Hey Siri, what's the latest weather?" Siri understands their command and retrieves the information by searching on the Internet.

Natural language generation (NLG) enables computers to produce human language so that people can understand computers. After Siri performed a search of the latest weather, it replies with an answer such as the following example: "it's currently clear and 28 degrees in Philadelphia. Expect partly cloudy skies starting tonight. Today's high will be 33 degrees, and the low will be 23 degrees". Siri understood that the user was asking it to look up the weather conditions at a specific location and time, and then returned the results in spoken English words. NLG can also convert data visualizations, such as charts and graphs, into a verbal description that can be understood by humans (CPA Canada & AICPA, 2019).

The potential for using NLP in accounting is substantial, as it can be used to process and analyze large amounts of data. NLP has been used to analyze various textual documents related to corporate financial performance and compliance with accounting standards and regulations (Fisher et al., 2016). Text mining uses NLP to extract meaning from textual data. Applications of NLP include text mining components such as semantics analysis, text classification, text summarization, and text translation. Additional applications include speech recognition, question-answering systems, and chatbots.

Data Mining

Data mining is a process of analyzing large data sets (i.e., "big data") to discover previously unknown patterns or relationships. Data mining tools are typically applied to structured data, that is, highly formatted data contained in relational databases such as in an ERP system and, therefore, can be very helpful for accountants.

As illustrated in Figure 1.2, data mining intersects with but is not considered a subfield of AI. As computer scientist Xavier Amatriain notes, "machine learning can be used for data. However, data mining can use other techniques on top of machine learning" (Amatriain, 2016, para. 5).

Like machine learning, data mining relies on reading large amounts of data to discover patterns and arrive at conclusions. However, technology expert Bernard Marr identified notable differences between data mining and machine learning. First, data mining looks for patterns that already exist in historical data, whereas ML attempts to predict future outcomes based on the given data. Second, the rules or patterns are unknown at the beginning of the data mining process, whereas the rules are programmed into the computer to understand the data with machine learning. Third, data mining relies on human intervention throughout the process, whereas much of the learning with ML is automatic. Finally, data mining uses an existing data set, such as a data warehouse, whereas ML learns from a training data set and then makes predictions using new data sets (Marr, n.d.).

By using data mining techniques on general ledger transactions, accountants can potentially unlock valuable insights and improve decision-making. For example, auditors can use data mining to help detect fraudulent purchases or outlier transactions that require further investigation. Management accountants can use data mining to assess the financial risk of a business entity, such as "trading partners, corporate affiliates, investment partners, and takeover targets" (Calderon et al., 2003, p. 7).

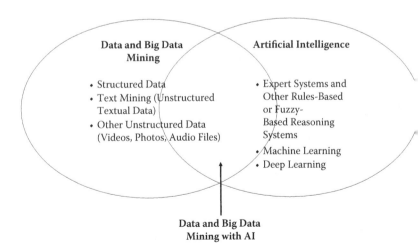

Figure 1.2 Relationship between (big) data mining and AI.

Text Mining

Text mining is a process of extracting information from various text sources (such as Word documents, PDF files, social media posts, emails, websites, articles, XML files, and others) to discover patterns, trends, and themes. The text found in these documents is typically unstructured, that is, they are not in a predefined format that can be analyzed through data analytics software such as IDEA or ACL. Text mining is performed in two steps: 1) imposing structure on the text data sources and then 2) using data mining techniques to extract relevant information (Sharda et al., 2014).

Text mining is useful in fields that have a large amount of textual data, as is the case with accounting. For example, auditors review contracts, invoices, legal letters, SEC filings, earnings, conference calls, news articles, and much more.

Professor Aldhizer (2017) of Wake Forest University suggests that forensic and audit practices consider using text analytics for high-risk engagements. Aldhizer notes that text analytics could be used for concept extraction to identify incriminating words from social media posts and emails. Text mining could be used to ensure proper reporting under lease and revenue recognition (Iowa State University, n.d.).

Robotic Process Automation (RPA) and AI

Although RPA is not considered a form of AI by some experts (CPA Canada & AICPA, 2019), this technology enables machines to perform functions usually carried out by humans. Firms are using RPA, coupled with AI capabilities, to increase productivity and performance. Thus, accountants need to understand what RPA is and how it can be combined with AI technologies. **Robotic process automation (RPA)** is a software application (robot or bot) that automates a business process by replicating the actions of humans performing tasks within digital systems, such as manipulating or transferring data. In many cases, the automation involves minimal coding and is typically activated by using a smart screen recording. Keep in mind that these robots are not physical steel machines found in the old science-fiction movies or television shows. RPA lends itself well to high-volume and repeatable tasks traditionally performed by humans. For example, RPA can be used to process bulk transactions, such as processing vendor invoices for payment.

By using RPA, businesses can achieve increased productivity and accuracy at a lower cost. The exponential growth in RPA adoption has been facilitated by the availability of software providers such as UiPath, Automation Anywhere, and BluePrism. Many RPA providers will allow individuals to have a limited version of their software to begin building bots. Examples of RPA in accounting include performing bank reconciliations, automating cash applications, and tracking accounts payable.

Application Programming Interfaces (API) and AI

An **application programming interface (API)** is a set of functions or rules that facilitates communication between applications, databases, and devices. An analogy to understand how an API works is a restaurant waiter who takes an order relays it to the kitchen and then returns the prepared food to the customer. APIs are like digital messengers – they allow the weather app on your phone to transmit and retrieve information from a third-party app such as the Weather Channel. As another example, APIs enable customers to purchase movie tickets through a site like Fandango by signing into their Facebook or Google accounts.

APIs are used extensively by AI and ML programmers. For example, Google's Prediction API provides cloud-based access to machine learning, natural language processing, recommendation engines, pattern recognition, and prediction services (Rizk, 2018). In a blog post entitled "Top 20 APIs You Should Know in AI and Machine Learning," Oleksii Kharkovyna (2019) notes that his preferred APIs are most suitable for AI and ML purposes. BigML, for example, uses APIs to create data sets, models, and predictions that use ML technology. As another example, Anaconda Enterprise is a data science platform that uses APIs to deploy machine learning models.

Best Programming Languages Accountants Should Learn for Artificial Intelligence Applications

Accountants with a strong technical background in programming languages will be best positioned to work with data scientists in implementing AI initiatives. For those do-it-yourself accountants who may want to customize AI technologies to solve applications, learning a programming language will be quite useful. Proficiency with popular open-source programming tools for AI, such as Python and R, will enable accountants to customize AI applications to suit the unique business needs of their firms or clients. Other tools, such as SQL and

NoSQL, will be useful for retrieving, editing, and manipulating data to be used with AI applications.

Accountants without a strong background in programming languages can also help develop AI-enabled applications by using "no-code" and "low-code" platforms. These platforms use drag-and-drop editors for application development rather than traditional coding languages. Some of the world's leading technology companies offer these solutions. For example, the "Create ML" application by Apple allows users to develop and train ML models using different datasets. Google's AI Platform supports "Kubeflow", their open-source application that enables developers to build AI/ML projects. Lastly, Microsoft's Cognitive Toolkit "CNTK" enables applications built for the Azure platform and allows users to develop customized applications for computer vision, natural language understanding, facial recognition, and prediction models. No-code and low-code tools are undoubtedly useful for accountants in implementing AI initiatives.

Notes

1 As used throughout this book, "KMPG" refers to KPMG International Cooperative ("KPMG International"). Member firms of the KPMG network of independent firms are affiliated with KPMG International. KPMG International provides no client services.
2 As used throughout this book, "Deloitte" means Deloitte & Touche LLP, a subsidiary of Deloitte LLP. Please see www.deloitte.com/us/about for a detailed description of the legal structure. Certain services may not be available to attest clients under the rules and regulations of public accounting.
3 As used throughout this book, "KMPG" refers to KPMG International Cooperative ("KPMG International"). Member firms of the KPMG network of independent firms are affiliated with KPMG International. KPMG International provides no client services.

References

Aldhizer, G. R. (2017). Visual and text analytics. *The CPA Journal, 87*(6), 30–33. https://www.cpajournal.com/2017/06/20/visual-text-analytics/.
Amatriain, X. (2016, January 14). *What's the relationship between machine learning and data mining?* Medium. https://medium.com/@xamat/what-s-the-relationship-between-machine-learning-and-data-mining-8c8675966615.
Bottou, L. (2014). From machine learning to machine reasoning: An essay. *Machine Learning, 94*(2), 133–149. https://doi.org/10.1007/s10994-013-5335-x.
Bringsjord, S., & Govindarajulu, N. S. (2018). Artificial intelligence. *The Stanford Encyclopedia of Philosophy* (Summer 2020 Edition). *Edward N. Zalta.* https://plato.stanford.edu/entries/artificial-intelligence/#HistAI.

Burns, M. B., & Igou, A. (2019). "Alexa, write an audit opinion": Adopting intelligent virtual assistants in accounting workplaces. *Journal of Emerging Technologies in Accounting, 16*(1), 81–92. https://doi.org/10.2308/jeta-52424.

Calderon, T. G., Cleh, J. J., & Kim, I. W. (2003). How large corporations use data mining to create value. *Management Accounting Quarterly, 3*(4), 1–12.

Camhi, J., & Pandolh, S. (2017, April 17). *Machine learning driving innovation at Amazon.* Business Insider. https://www.businessinsider.com/machine-learning-driving-innovation-at-amazon-2017-4.

Colom , R, Karama , S, Jung , RE, & Haier , RJ (2010). Human intelligence and brain networks. *Dialogues Clin Neurosci, 12*(4), 489–501.

CPA Canada, & AICPA. (2019). *A CPA' s Introduction to AI: From Algorithms to Deep Learning, What You Need to Know.* CPA Canada. https://www.cpacanada.ca/en/business-and-accounting-resources/other-general-business-topics/information-management-and-technology/publications/a-cpa-introduction-to-ai.

Deloitte. (2015). *Deloitte wins 'Audit Innovation of the Year' at 2015 International Accounting Bulletin awards.* https://www2.deloitte.com/ch/en/pages/audit/articles/deloitte-wins-iab-audit-innovation-award.html.

Dobrev, D. (2012). A definition of artificial intelligence. *Mathematica Balkanica, New Series, 19*, 1–7.

Duffy, N. (2019, August 8). *How AI is transforming business right now.* EY. https://www.ey.com/en_us/innovation/how-ai-is-transforming-business-right-now.

Fisher, I. E., Garnsey, M. R., & Hughes, M. E. (2016). Natural language processing in accounting, auditing, and finance: A synthesis of the literature with a roadmap for future research. *Intelligent Systems in Accounting, Finance, and Management, 23*(3), 157–214. https://doi.org/10.1002/isaf.1386.

ICAEW. (2017). *Artificial intelligence and the future of accountancy.* https://www.icaew.com/-/media/corporate/files/technical/information-technology/thought-leadership/artificial-intelligence-report.ashx.

Iowa State University. (n.d.). *Textual Analytics for Accounting and Auditing.* https://www.ivybusiness.iastate.edu/files/2018/12/Janvrin-Textual-Analysis-Presentation-Dec-14-2018.pdf.

Jajal, T. (2018, May 21). *Distinguishing between Narrow AI, General AI, and Super AI.* Medium. https://medium.com/@tjajal/distinguishing-between-narrow-ai-general-ai-and-super-ai-a4bc44172e22.

Kharkovyna, O. (2019, March 11). *Top 20 APIs you should know in AI and Machine Learning.* Towards Data Science. https://towardsdatascience.com/top-20-apis-you-should-know-in-ai-and-machine-learning-8e08515198b3.

Marr, B. (n.d.). What is the difference between data mining and machine learning? Bernard Marr & Co. https://bernardmarr.com/default.asp?contentID=1741#:~:text=Data%20mining%20is%20used%20on,predictions%20about%20new%20data%20sets.

Merriam-Webster. (2020). Intelligence. In *Merriam-Webster.com dictionary*. https://www.merriam-webster.com/dictionary/intelligence.

Negnevitsky, M. (2011). *Artificial Intelligence: A guide to intelligent systems* (3rd ed.). Addison-Wesley, an imprint of Pearson.

New York State Society of CPAs. (2015). Technology in accounting history. *CPA Journal, 85*(11), 16–17. https://www.cpajournal.com/2017/11/30/technology-accounting-history/.

Pathak, J., Vidyarthi, N., & Summers, S. L. (2005). A fuzzy-based algorithm for auditors to detect elements of fraud in settled insurance claims. *Managerial Auditing Journal, 20*(6), 632–644. https://doi.org/10.1108/02686900510606119.

Pepe, A. A. (2011, April 19). *The evolution of technology for the accounting profession*. CPA Practice Advisor. http://www.cpapracticeadvisor.com/article/10263076/the-evolution-of-technology-for-the-accounting-profession.

Rizk, A. (2018, January 23). *How API and artificial intelligence can be complementary?* API Friends. https://apifriends.com/api-management/api-and-artificial-intelligence/.

Russell, S., & Norvig, P. (2010). *Artificial intelligence – A modern approach*. Prentice-Hall.

Samuel, J. (2018, March 21). *KPMG applying IBM artificial intelligence to help businesses efficiently meet IFRS 16 lease account requirements*. KPMG. https://home.kpmg/xx/en/home/media/press-releases/2018/03/kpmg-applying-ibm-ai-to-help-businesses-meet-ifrs-16.html.

Schwab, K. (2017). *The fourth industrial revolution*. Crown Business.

Sharda, R., Delen, D., & Turban, E. (2014). *Business intelligence* (3rd ed.). Pearson.

Siegel, J., Shim, J., Walker, J., Qureshi, A., O'Callaghan, S., & Koku, P. (2003). *The artificial intelligence handbook: Business applications in accounting, banking, finance, management, and marketing*. South-Western, a division of Thomson Learning.

Sun, T. S. (2019). Applying deep learning to audit procedures: An illustrative framework. *Accounting Horizons, 33*(3), 89–109. https://doi.org/10.2308/acch-52455.

The Mathworks & MATLAB. (2018). *Introducing Deep Learning with MATLAB: What is Deep Learning?* https://www.mathworks.com/content/dam/mathworks/ebook/gated/80879v00_Deep_Learning_ebook.pdf.

Untapped Editorial Team. (2018, August 29). *The history of accounting – From record keeping to artificial intelligence discover how the history of accounting evolved*. Medius. https://www.mediusflow.com/en/untapped/articles/people/history-of-accounting.

Vien, C. (Host). (2018, July 30). *Using drones to enhance audits* [Audio Podcast]. *Journal of Accountancy*. https://www.journalofaccountancy.com/podcast/using-drones-to-enhance-audits.html.

Walch, K. (2019, October 4). *Rethinking weak vs. strong AI*. Forbes. https://www.forbes.com/sites/cognitiveworld/2019/10/04/rethinking-weak-vs-strong-ai/#4cf807ab6da3.

Weiner, I. B., & Freedheim, D. K. (2013). *Handbook of psychology, history of psychology* (2nd ed.). John Wiley & Sons.

Wittbold, K. A., Carroll, C., Iansiti, M., Zhang, H. M., & Landman, A. B. (2020). *How hospitals are using AI to Battle Covid-19.* Harvard Business Review. https://hbr.org/2020/04/how-hospitals-are-using-ai-to-battle-covid-19.

Yang, D. C., & Vasarhelyi, M. (1993). The application of expert systems in libraries. *The Journal of Academic Librarianship, 19*(1), 45–46. https://doi.org/10.1016/0099-1333(93)90774-y.

Yao, M., Jia, M., & Zhou, A. (2018). *Applied artificial intelligence: A handbook for business leaders* (N. Zhang, Ed.). TOPBOTS Inc.

2 Applications of AI in Accounting

According to a survey by the World Economic Forum, most executives from 151 financial institutions in 33 countries expect that AI will become essential to their business within two years (World Economic Forum, 2020). Although AI receives much attention in corporate news, there is a large gap between business leaders who believe that AI can provide their companies with a competitive advantage versus those who are already using it. In a global survey of over 3,000 executives by the *MIT Sloan Management Review* (in collaboration with the Boston Consulting Group), nearly 85% of respondents reported that they expect AI-enabled technology to provide a competitive advantage for their firms. However, less than 39% reported having an AI strategy in place, and only 5% extensively reported having incorporated AI into their products and services (Ransbotham et al., 2017). This study exemplifies the current environment for AI: business leaders recognize the potential benefits that AI can bring, but widespread adoption has yet to be achieved. The opportunity for accountants to leverage AI for business is tremendous.

The power of present-day AI technology far exceeds accountants' traditional technological toolkits (e.g., electronic spreadsheets, general ledger software, and tax compliance programs), especially when combined with advanced data analytics. Artificial intelligence has three broad applications for business: (1) to better understand and interact with customers, (2) to offer more intelligent products and services, and (3) to improve and automate business processes (Marr & Ward, 2019). Because accounting is a highly process-oriented discipline, many of the current use cases automate traditional accounting functions. Accountants who understand how AI is currently being used in practice are well-positioned to suggest other possible AI-enabled solutions to their unique business challenges. To this end, this chapter provides examples of how AI can be deployed across various sectors of the accounting industry, including financial accounting, management accounting, audit, tax, and advisory services.

Financial Accounting Applications

Cash and Account Reconciliations

Accountants understand that performing bank reconciliation serves as a critical detective control to help safeguard cash and improve the accuracy of reported accounting information. However, completing traditional bank reconciliation can be time-consuming, especially for mid-size to large companies with multiple accounts at various institutions. Common errors encountered during the bank reconciliation process include duplicate entries, different data formats between systems (e.g., bank portal versus ERP system), and human-generated data entry errors (e.g., misspellings, character spacing) (Sigma IQ, 2019). Automating the bank reconciliation process with artificial intelligence promises to save time and improve accuracy for accounting departments.

Expert Systems (ES) are well suited for bank reconciliations because the rules are straightforward and do not change over time (Siegel et al., 2003). Nolan Business Solutions, an international firm with headquarters in the UK, uses an ES called Advanced Bank Reconciliation (ABR) that works with NetSuite, a leading provider of cloud-based services including accounting and ERP systems. ABR imports transactions from the bank, then automatically matches transactions based on user-defined rules, and finally generates reports on un-reconciled transactions (Nolan Business Solutions, n.d.). The ABR interface allows users to classify any remaining unmatched transactions, significantly reducing the amount of time that an employee would spend manually matching the transactions. After the reconciliation is completed, the transactions are saved to the hard drive or network. The transactions can be viewed or examined later for audit purposes.

The latest AI technologies, such as machine learning (ML), can further enhance the automation of account reconciliation. For example, Sigma IQ is a software provider that specializes in using machine learning to automate the account reconciliation process. Its cloud-based AI platform goes beyond a rule-based Expert System by deploying algorithms to develop a nuanced understanding of how to resolve common issues. In this way, ML can continuously learn each time that a human makes a mistake and include that error in its processing for future reconciliations. As such, ML can significantly improve the account reconciliation process and save companies hundreds of manual hours in processing time (Sigma IQ, 2019). ML can also identify and prioritize reconciling items that might need further investigation by staff accountants.

Receivables and Sales

The cash application process requires accounts receivable staff to match incoming payments to outstanding invoices. This time-consuming process is costly and prone to errors, especially when dealing with many customers and high volume transactions. This process has become even more complicated due to the variety of payment methods available (e.g., check, ACH, wire transfers, credit card payments, PayPal, Venmo, etc.). Additional problems can result from missing or incorrect reference numbers, combined or partial payments, and invoices in different languages and currencies (Sinha & Davis, 2018).

AI has helped firms to automate processes that match payments and remittances at much faster speeds than can be done manually, effectively reducing the number of staff hours and costs associated with this activity. ES can be used to validate customer orders, grant credit based on pre-defined criteria, automatically invoice, and post-sales entries to subsidiary ledgers (Siegel et al., 2003).

More recent developments in AI and ML technologies are providing additional efficiencies and cost reductions. For example, Fifth Third Bank offers a service, called Expert AR Receivables Matching, which integrates with ERP systems to reduce the cost and risk of manually matching and posting receivables (Fifth Third Bank, n.d.). The service works by collecting all payments into a centralized location and then using ML to match and post A/R transactions. Once a payment exception from a customer is manually validated, the system learns to recognize incoming payments in the same format to increase the chance that it is processed without exceptions. Unmatched payments can be reconciled with a single click using a matching algorithm.

Citi is another bank leading the industry in deploying AI to manage their receivables. They developed a solution called Citi® Smart Match. Smart Match uses AI to read a variety of sources of remittance information (e.g., emails, email attachments, faxes, remittance advice, web portals, and electronic data interchanges (EDI)). The purpose is to identify and extract the most important payment details (Sinha & Davis, 2018). The technology then transforms the extracted data into a format that can be used for creating structured remittance data files. The remittance file is then matched against the company's outstanding receivables, and the results are transmitted to the company's ERP system "on a straight-through basis to achieve end-to-end reconciliation" (Sinha & Davis, 2018, p. 2).

The Citi® Smart Match system identifies unmatched items and generates a report in much less time than it would take a human to complete. A/R specialists can then use the report to manually input missing information or correct erroneous data. ML is used to learn from each human interaction and resolve future unmatched items on its own. It typically takes three to four months for the system to be trained, and then it can achieve straight-through reconciliation rates near 90%, reducing the amount of time spent by staff updating errors by 80% (Sinha & Davis, 2018). Thus, the amount of errors decreases, operational efficiency increases, and payments are posted faster, freeing up A/R staff to focus on the collection of valid cash items. Performance metrics such as Days Sales Outstanding (DSO) decreases, and the working capital improves.

Finally, another example is HighRadius Corporation, a provider of AI software for accounts receivable operations, including A/R automation, predictive capabilities (cash forecasting), and analytics. HighRadius asserts that its cloud-based platform is used by more than 200 Fortune 1,000 Companies, including global firms such as Starbucks, 3M, and Johnson and Johnson (HighRadius, n.d.). One of the case studies featured by HighRadius includes Express Employment Professionals, a staffing and recruiting company in North America. Before using HighRadius, Express Employment faced several challenges related to its A/R operations, including high fees for lockbox services at three banks averaging over $7,000 per month in total. The company processed 25,000 invoices per week, 4,500 line-items per day, and 3,000 payments per day. Furthermore, the ACH payment process was 100% manual, and payments were de-coupled from remittance sources such as emails, portals, and EDI files. By using HighRadius's AI platform, Express Employment achieved 85% automation for checks and ACH transactions and saved $84,000 in annual lockbox fees (Richards, n.d.).

Inventory

Sound inventory management is an essential ingredient for success in merchandising and manufacturing companies. The challenge for managers is to strike the right balance between maintaining enough stock to meet demand and limiting excess inventory, which can deplete cash reserves and increase storage and carrying costs. Unfortunately, the requirements for inventory management are highly dynamic, featuring demand variations, seasonal fluctuations, and stock-outs (Patil & Divekar, 2014). For some companies, an outdated or manual inventory management system can make managers unaware of inventory levels and thereby result in the mismanagement of inventory space and people (APS Fulfillment Inc., 2018).

The two critical implementations of AI for inventory management systems are (1) demand prediction for inventory management, and (2) reinforcement learning for full inventory management (Hamilton, 2018). Demand prediction involves the development of a time series model that can forecast demand across all items in inventory by incorporating external data sources such as weather. Reinforcement learning is a more advanced approach where the system not only makes predictions about inventory levels but also takes actions to order inventory automatically.

Amazon is a pioneer in using AI to streamline various parts of its operations. The company has implemented AI for inventory management at an unprecedented scale (Hamilton, 2018). Specifically, Amazon uses AI to forecast consumer demand, supplier backorders, warehouse optimization, and stock level optimization. AI-enabled robots allowed Amazon to increase efficiency and safety at its fulfillment centers and to store 40% more inventory. As a result, Amazon is better equipped to satisfy its Amazon Prime offerings and other deliveries, is less likely to run out of stock, and is able to deliver a faster and more consistent customer experience (About Amazon Staff, 2019).

AI can be used to manage inventory levels in real-time by analyzing large amounts of data from various sources, including ERP systems and the Internet. In a recent blog post, Alasdair Hamilton (2018), CEO of AI research firm Remi AI, emphasized the profound impact that AI can have on inventory management:

"We are on the verge of a major upheaval in the way inventory is managed. This revolution is a result of the availability of the huge amounts of real-time data that are now routinely generated on the Internet and through the interconnected world of enterprise software systems and smart products" (para. 5)

Effective application of AI for inventory management can help organizations optimize inventory levels, minimize storage costs, and increase profitability.

Accounts Payable

The accounts payable (A/P) process involves matching invoices to supporting documents, such as purchase orders and contracts. Matching is necessary to ensure that payments are authorized for the correct amount and in compliance with purchasing contracts and that they are encoded correctly in the general ledger. Many companies rely on an outdated analog system for matching paper invoices to other paper source documents. According to research firm Gartner, only about 10% of businesses worldwide receive invoices in electronic form. The lack of electronic invoices suggests an incredible opportunity exists in A/P to increase efficiency and effectiveness through the targeted application of AI services. Specifically, invoice automation combined with an AI-powered matching engine can dramatically reduce manual work, improve process cycle times, and increase the return of investment (Keck et al., 2019).

Machine learning algorithms combined with optical character recognition (OCR) can be used to automate the A/P process by extracting data from receipts and invoices and then classifying the type of expense in the general ledger (Vordenbaeumen, 2019). Unfortunately, current accounts payable invoice automation (APIA) initiatives tend only to address document digitization, largely ignoring the matching component (Keck et al., 2019). Gartner provides several examples of common invoice mismatches that automation can address, some of which include pricing discrepancies, unknown or not identifiable suppliers, and invoice quantities that do not match the purchase order (Keck et al., 2019).

Invoice automation can be supplemented with a machine learning engine to significantly improve match rates. These enhanced AI systems perform better than an off-the-shelf, rules-based expert systems engine. AI-enabled APIA can perform sophisticated matching when an invoice does not initially have a match.

It is straightforward to realize the potency of AI in A/P. The first step is to receive invoices in digital form. The next step is to automatically match invoices to the purchase order using AI. When an invoice does not have a matching purchase order (PO), such as with utility bills and taxes, AI can learn to approve invoices without POs by analyzing contracts and expense categories that were previously approved for payment without a matching PO. Gartner explains that an APIA solution should not only understand the issue with the invoice but also be able to identify the appropriate person to resolve the problem (Keck et al., 2019). Finally, Gartner recommends that APIA systems should prioritize workflows so that high-value invoices and those close to payment or discount dates are flagged over others to ensure a timely resolution.

Gartner provides a sample of APIA vendors on the market, including Medius, The Shelby Group, Basware, Esker, and AvidXchange. For example, Medius developed an APIA solution called MediusFlow AP. It uses OCR and Intelligent Data Capture (IDC) to digitally capture information such as the purchase order number, amount, and date. It then uses a template to automatically enter the data into the A/P system for processing. According to the vendor, companies that use their solution process up to 97% of their invoices via a fully automated and touch-free workflow (Medius Software Inc., n.d.).

Management Accounting Applications

Management accountants use their knowledge and expertise to support business planning, controlling, and decision making (Garrison et al., 2018). In their Managerial Accounting book, researcher Garrison et al. (2018) said that "the most basic managerial skill is the ability to make intelligent, data-driven decisions" (p. 4). The amount and types of data that are generated each day continue to accelerate, thus, the possibilities to use AI for management accounting are significant. AI technology can assist management accountants with data analysis to generate insights, improve decision-making, increase productivity, and enhance operational performance.

Manufacturers with a large number of long-term assets are also exploring ways in which AI can enhance operations and improve profitability. A study from McKinsey found that AI technologies can optimize production processes that traditionally rely on human operators' experience, intuition, and judgment (Charalambous et al., 2019). McKinsey worked with a cement company client to integrate AI to install real-time asset optimizers by capturing millions of lines of data from hundreds of process variables and analyzing said data using advanced analytics tools. The study found that profits improved within a few weeks of implementation. After eight months, the AI-enabled asset optimizer improved operational performance by 11.6% versus the analog processes (Charalambous et al., 2019). In short, the introduction of AI improved results without requiring capital-intensive equipment upgrades.

AI has also been used to support decision-making and enhance operational performance in the parcel delivery industry. In Japan, for example, a surge in online shopping and a shortage of drivers has strained the parcel delivery industry (Tsukimori, 2020). In response, Japan Data Science Consortium (JDSC) developed its own AI patent that analyzes household electricity data to calculate whether someone is likely to be home during the package delivery period. The idea was simple: When electricity usage is high, someone is likely to be home to receive a package, effectively avoiding the added costs and time associated with re-delivery of the package. Based on a pilot study conducted in 2018, the rate of re-deliveries was reduced by 90%.

The analysis produced by AI could be incorporated into a balanced scorecard (BSC). The BSC consists of an integrated set of performance measures that include four perspectives that are directly linked to the company's strategy: (1) financial, (2) customer, (3) internal business processes and (4) learning and growth (Kaplan & Norton, 1992).

From a financial perspective, management accountants would become responsible for capturing the costs associated with AI initiatives to ensure cost-effectiveness. Additional financial performance indicators, such as ROI and other profitability measures, could be tracked. From the customer handling perspective, managers could track satisfaction through surveys after implementing AI initiatives. Managers could also measure how the percentage of customers changes (decreasing, increasing, or staying the same) after AI implementation. From the internal business processes perspective, managers could track whether their organization has improved key business processes by addressing the following kinds of questions: Are standard cost variances decreasing because of using AI? Is the service delivery time decreasing? From the learning and growth perspective, managers could monitor how the company leveraged AI to change and improve its competencies. For example, are employees being adequately trained on how to fully take advantage of all the benefits of AI in their respective responsibility area?

Audit Applications

Auditors play a critical role in our society by providing assurance services related to financial statements and internal controls. Auditors render an opinion after accumulating and evaluating evidence (i.e., data). Given the ability of AI systems to analyze vast amounts of structured and unstructured data, AI can be employed in all phases of a financial statement audit – from planning, data gathering in fieldwork, completing the audit, and issuing the final audit opinion.

Baldwin et al. (2006) documented several applications of AI for auditing tasks. For example, neural networks have been used for performing analytical review procedures and risk assessments. AI algorithms can be used to assist with classification tasks for transactions (e.g., collectible debt vs. bad debt, legitimate transaction vs.

unauthorized). ES has been used for materiality assessments, internal control evaluations, and going concern judgments.

Although many examples of the applications of AI in audit mentioned in the literature are initiatives from large firms, small firms can also take advantage of AI for audits. For instance, Garbelman Winslow CPAs, a small firm based in Marlboro, Maryland, uses an AI platform called Ai Auditor developed by MindBridge Analytics to identify high-risk transactions during the audit planning process. Specifically, the firm uses machine learning algorithms to analyze the entire general ledger. The AI platform then compares the general ledger data against benchmarks to group the transactions into three risk categories: low risk, medium risk, and high risk. As Samantha Bowling (2019), partner at Garbelman Winslow CPAs, stated in her article: "AI is absolutely more comprehensive; it alerts us when things don't look right and tells us where to start and where our risk is going to be. It shows the risk at the transaction level" (para. 3).

Bowling also stated that small public accounting firms could implement the technology for less than $10,000, but the price depends on the size of the firm. In her article, Bowling describes that because the system is cloud-based, she can connect her QuickBooks clients directly to the MindBridge platform and upload the entire general ledger. The software then categorizes the transactions into the different risk buckets at the transaction level. Bowling notes that using AI gives their firm a competitive advantage over firms that use traditional sampling. She also uses MindBridge when determining whether to accept or reject a client and in pricing their services. If a client has several risky transactions, she can either reject or raise the price appropriately to account for the increased risk.

Given the capabilities of AI for the audit function, it is no surprise that the world's largest accounting firms, including the Big 4, have invested hundreds of millions of dollars in various AI-related technologies (Rapoport, 2016). KPMG, for example, uses Clara, an audit platform that integrates AI and automation to read and extract data from both structured data (e.g., general ledger) and unstructured source documents (e.g., paper-based invoices, emails, instant messages, social media). The data is then reconciled to company records, and any discrepancies are flagged for review by humans. A task that originally took several hours is reduced to several minutes, freeing up the audit team to focus on other areas of higher risk (KPMG, 2019).

Deloitte's Argus tool uses machine learning and natural language processing to extract key accounting information from just about any type of electronic document (e.g., sales agreements, leasing and derivative contracts, invoices, meetings minutes, and legal letters to improve the quality and efficiency of an audit) (Deloitte, 2015). Argus can review a population of documents, such as leases, and then uses ML to isolate and visualize any modifications to a contract that deviated from a standard contract, and then export the information into a workpaper for additional analysis by the auditor (Raphael, 2017).

EY uses natural language processing to analyze lengthy text documents such as legal contracts and leases to determine compliance with accounting standards (Nickerson, 2019). EY developed a tool called EY Document Intelligence, which uses natural language processing to review thousands of contracts as part of an audit engagement. Traditionally, auditors might manually review a single contract that contained hundreds of pages to identify key terms. The EY Document Intelligence tool analyzes a much larger volume of contracts in less time with greater accuracy. For example, in analyzing a lease agreement, the EY tool extracts the commencement date, lease amounts, and any related clauses. The auditor then selects the most relevant values using their professional judgment (Duffy, 2019). The tool continues to learn each time that it interacts with an EY auditor, becoming more effective over time. EY notes that deep learning will enable machines to analyze large amounts of unstructured data such as emails, social media posts, and conference call audio files.

PwC[1] partnered with H2O.ai, an AI firm based in the Silicon Valley, to build GL.ai which is a bot that analyzes "billions of data points in milliseconds, seeing what humans [cannot], and applying judgment to detect anomalies in the general ledger" (PwC, n.d., para. 1). The algorithm is designed to replicate the decision making process of an experienced auditor by analyzing all transactions in the general ledger. The more tasks the AI tool analyzes, the smarter it becomes. PwC notes that using GL.ai has increased efficiency and effectiveness, completing the analysis in less time than it would take a human auditor, while also providing more significant insights. This allows auditors to focus on areas with the most significant risk.

Tax Applications

AI can be utilized for a variety of tax functions. For example, AI can be used for extracting critical data from tax documents, classifying sensitive transactions, identifying possible deductions and tax credits, comparing pricing structures for transfer pricing, and tax forecasting (Van Volkenburgh, 2019).

Technology services firm CrowdReason provides software called MetaTaskerPT to classify documents by asking human workers to identify the document type. The software recognizes a correct answer when there is consensus by three separate people. A similar process is used for defining the taxonomy of a document by asking questions such as: Is there an account number? How many payments on the tax bill? When is the due date? Much like other ML algorithms, the more data MetaTaskerPT analyzes, the better able it is to recognize documents.

Once the system understands the document, it can extract key information and automatically input it into a software system (Van Volkenburgh, 2019). AI can be used for classifying tax-sensitive transactions that generally take a lot of time for human staff to accomplish. For example, algorithms can be used to identify assets that are incorrectly booked to accounts based on historical classifications made by staff. By using machine learning, the number of manual reviews can be reduced from 50,000 transactions per year to less than 300 (Van Volkenburgh, 2019).

AI can also be used to review tax notices received from various tax jurisdictions to determine if they are informational or require action. ML can be used by tax agencies for predictive modeling to identify potential fraud or tax avoidance. Given how lengthy and complicated the Internal Revenue Code is, AI is well suited for identifying possible deductions and tax credits. For example, H&R Block uses IBM's Watson system as part of its questionnaire engine.

Deloitte uses AI for a variety of tax applications. For example, the firm uses natural language generators in its tax practice to provide targeted financial advice (Nickerson, 2019). It also uses a supervised machine learning tool with NLP to automatically extract clauses from legal documents such as contracts and deeds. It can review high volumes of trust agreements to automatically classify the type of trust for tax purposes, saving tax professionals a multitude of work hours each year.

Furthermore, Deloitte has a global practice that specializes in recovering refunds related to indirect taxes, such as sales taxes or value-added tax (VAT). Due to the complexity of tax laws in various jurisdictions and the vast volume of data, indirect tax recovery is a challenge. Deloitte uses CognitiveTax Insight™ (CogTax) for indirect tax recovery. CogTax can analyze the full population of accounts payable transactions by applying optical character recognition (OCR), machine learning algorithms, and analytics to identify overpayments and reduce the potential for over or underpayments in the future (Deloitte, 2019).

EY developed a tool called the capital allowances automated review tool (CAART), which uses machine learning to assist with identifying potential allowances (i.e., tax relief) that are often overlooked (Duffy, 2019). The CAART tool analyzes large volumes of fixed asset cost data (e.g., buildings under construction) at rates much faster than humans to assign the correct tax treatment. This analysis requires an understanding of tax legislation, case law, and construction terminology. The CAART tool uses ML to learn the relationship between text descriptions and the corresponding tax treatment. The raw data comes from the client's accounting system or from external cost consultants and is then uploaded into CAART. This tool then predicts the tax treatment based on what it learned from the training data set (and this only takes a matter of seconds).

After the output is downloaded, CAART provides a probability score of citing how confident the system is that it predicted the correct answer. If necessary, corrections are made to the output, and once approved, the results can be included in the training data set so that the system learns and will have increased accuracy for the next case. The tool also has the capability and flexibility to be programmed with additional rules to accommodate legislation changes and "what if" scenarios.

The *Wall Street Journal* recently reported that governments around the world are increasingly using machine learning and data analytics to identify tax evaders, respond to inquiries, and generally become more efficient (Rubin, 2020). Brazil is using these technologies to detect anomalies, which has resulted in a 30% increase in inspections. Canada will be launching Charlie the Chatbot to respond to taxpayers' inquiries. In the United States, the Internal Revenue Service is using AI to examine notes recorded by IRS agents when responding to queries. The IRS also uses AI to determine the optimal combination of notices and contacts that are most likely to result in the taxpayer settling the amount owed. The IRS analyzes data from inside and outside the agency to identify thousands of high-income individuals who did not file returns. The article notes that the IRS criminal investigation unit uses Palantir Technologies, a data-mining firm, to identify potentially fraudulent cases.

Advisory Applications

In addition to accounting, audit, and tax services, many accounting professionals are involved in business advisory activities ranging from strategic finance consulting to internal audit and compliance services. Accountants may also use the various AI systems or kinds of AI tools mentioned earlier in their business advisory activities. There is also a plethora of AI tools that accountants may use as part of their IT audit engagements (e.g., IT risk and cybersecurity) and industry-specific consulting activities (e.g., anti-money laundering and other banking regulatory compliance).

As an illustration of the use of AI in advisory activities by accountants, KPMG's Advisory practice, in cooperation with IBM, uses a Contract Abstraction Tool (KCAT) to help clients comply with the IFRS 16 lease accounting standards. KCAT uses IBM Watson to assist with automating the contract data extraction process from any document (KPMG & IBM, 2017).

The challenge for clients of KPMG is ensuring that all leases are properly recognized on the balance sheet. Complicating factors include the sheer volume of leasing contracts, differences based on country of origin (different languages and currencies), and lack of a centralized department that handles leases (e.g., finance, IT, real estate, etc.) (KPMG & IBM, 2017). Leases that were previously not included on the balance sheet must now be capitalized according to the requirements of IFRS 16.

KCAT works by first converting PDF documents and image files into a machine-readable format. Next, the contracts are classified by type (e.g., real estate, IT, vehicles) and manually reviewed by KPMG staff. The last step ensures that certain attributes are extracted and transformed into a structured format and then imported into a lease accounting tool. The value-added here comes in the form of efficient and effective extraction of leasing contract data, classification and prioritization of contracts, and a significant reduction in the amount of staff involvement; moreover, all contract attributes are centrally available and linked to the original contract.

Conclusion

As the use cases in this chapter demonstrate, the accounting profession is beginning to use AI and ML to solve a variety of business problems. Computing power will continue to advance, more data will continue to be generated, and the cost of storing and analyzing data will likely continue to drop. The opportunities to use AI to solve new problems will only continue to rise, and adoption will become more widespread as time progresses.

Note

1 As used throughout this book, "PwC" refers to the US member firm or one of its subsidiaries or affiliates, and may sometimes refer to the PwC network. Each member firm is a separate legal entity. Please see www.pwc.com/structure for further details.

References

About Amazon Staff. (2019, July 24). *What robots do (and don't do) at Amazon fulfillment centers*. About Amazon. https://www.aboutamazon.com/amazon-fulfillment/our-innovation/what-robots-do-and-dont-do-at-amazon-fulfillment-centers/.

APS Fulfillment Inc. (2018, February 22). *Common challenges in real-time inventory management*. https://www.apsfulfillment.com/product-fulfillment-services/common-challenges-in-real-time-inventory-management/.

Baldwin, A. A., Brown, C. B., & Trinkle, B. S. (2006). Opportunities for Artificial intelligence development in the accounting domain: The case for auditing. *Intelligent Systems in Accounting, Finance, and Management*, *14*, 77–86. https://doi.org/10.1002/isaf.277.

Bowling, S. (2019). How we successfully implemented AI in audit. *Journal of Accountancy*. https://www.journalofaccountancy.com/issues/2019/jun/artificial-intelligence-in-audit.html.

Charalambous, E., Feldmann, R., Richter, G., & Schmitz, C. (2019, March 7). *AI in production: A game changer for manufacturers with heavy assets*. McKinsey. https://www.mckinsey.com/business-functions/mckinsey-analytics/our-insights/ai-in-production-a-game-changer-for-manufacturers-with-heavy-assets?cid=soc-app.

Deloitte. (2015). Deloitte *'Audit Innovation of the Year' at 2015 International Accounting Bulletin awards*. https://www2.deloitte.com/ch/en/pages/audit/articles/deloitte-wins-iab-audit-innovation-award.html.

Deloitte. (2019). *Deloitte uses AI to transform indirect tax recovery tax recovery*. https://www2.deloitte.com/us/en/pages/about-deloitte/articles/press-releases/deloitte-uses-ai-to-transform-indirect-tax-recovery.html.

Duffy, N. (2019, August 8). *How AI is transforming business right now*. EY. https://www.ey.com/en_us/innovation/how-ai-is-transforming-business-right-now.

Fifth Third Bank. (n.d.). *Fifth third bank expert AR receivables matching*. https://www.53.com/content/fifth-third/en/commercial-banking/treasury-management/expert-AR.html.

Garrison, R. H., Noreen, E. W., & Brewer, P. C. (2018). *Managerial accounting* (16th ed.). McGraw-Hill Irwin.

Hamilton, A. (2018, July 3). *Artificial intelligence for inventory management*. Medium. https://medium.com/@RemiStudios/artificial-intelligence-for-inventory-management-c8a9c0c2a694.

HighRadius. (n.d.). Retrieved March 3, 2020 from https://www.highradius.com/#product-section.

Kaplan, R. S., & Norton, D. P. (1992). The balanced scorecard: Measures that drive performance. *Harvard Business Review*, *70*(1), 71–79.

Keck, M., Sommers, K., & Abbabatulla, B. (2019, July 1). *Success with AP invoice automation requires more than paper to digital* (ID: G00391829). Retrieved from Gartner Database.

KPMG. (2019, February 18). *Intelligent automation tools in audit [Video]*. YouTube. https://www.youtube.com/watch?v=PXC9HS9yeg0&feature=youtu.be.

KPMG, & IBM. (2017). *Automated contract data extraction within the IFRS 16 lease framework*. KPMG. https://advisory.kpmg.us/content/dam/advisory/en/pdfs/automated-contract-data.pdf.

Marr, B., & Ward, M. (2019). *Artificial Intelligence in practice: How 50 Successful companies used AI and machine learning to solve problems*. Wiley.

Medius Software Inc. (n.d.). *Invoice matching*. MediusFlow AP. https://www.mediusflow.com/en/invoice-matching.

Nickerson, M. (2019, April). AI: New risks and rewards. *Strategic Finance*, 1–11. https://sfmagazine.com/post-entry/april-2019-ai-new-risks-and-rewards/.

Nolan Business Solutions. (n.d.). *Advanced bank reconciliation (ABR) for NetSuite*. http://www.nolanbusinesssolutions.com/us/files/Advanced-Bank-Reconciliation-for-NetSuite-Factsheet.pdf.

Patil, H., & Divekar, B. R. (2014). Inventory management challenges for B2C e-commerce retailers. *Procedia Economics and Finance, 11*(14), 561–571. https://doi.org/10.1016/s2212-5671(14)00221-4.

PwC. (n.d.). *Harnessing the power of AI to transform the detection of fraud and error*. https://www.pwc.com/gx/en/about/stories-from-across-the-world/harnessing-the-power-of-ai-to-transform-the-detection-of-fraud-and-error.html.

Ransbotham, S., Kiron, D., Gerbert, P., & Reeves, M. (2017). *Reshaping business with artificial intelligence. MIT Sloan Management Review and The Boston Consulting Group*. https://image-src.bcg.com/Images/Reshaping%20Business%20with%20Artificial%20Intelligence_tcm9-177882.pdf.

Raphael, J. (2017). Rethinking the audit. *Journal of Accountancy, 223*(4), 28–32. https://www.journalofaccountancy.com/issues/2017/apr/rethinking-the-audit.html.

Rapoport, M. (2016, Mar 08). CFO journal: *Auditors count on tech for backup. Wall Street Journal*, 1–3. Retrieved from http://libproxy.temple.edu/login?url=https://www-proquest-com.libproxy.temple.edu/docview/1771109214?accountid=14270.

Richards, A. (n.d.). *Error-free, same-day posting for over 25,000 invoices a week*. HighRadius. https://cdn2.hubspot.net/hubfs/190654/customer-success-story/ExpressEmployment.pdf.

Rubin, B. R. (2020). AI comes to the tax code. *Wall Street Journal*. https://www.wsj.com/articles/ai-comes-to-the-tax-code-11582713000.

Siegel, J., Shim, J., Walker, J., Qureshi, A., O'Callaghan, S., & Koku, P. (2003). *The artificial intelligence handbook: Business applications in accounting, banking, finance, management, and marketing*. South-Western, a division of Thomson Learning.

Sigma IQ. (2019, June 4). *Automated bank reconciliations through RPA & machine learning*. https://www.sigmaiq.com/finance-blog/automating-bank-reconciliations-through-rpa-machine-learning.

Sinha, A., & Davis, L. (2018). *Straight-through receivables reconciliations: AI and machine learning boost efficiency and working capital.* CitiBank. https://www.citibank.com/tts/solutions/receivables/assets/docs/AI-Machine-Learning.pdf.

Tsukimori, O. (2020, February 26). *Harnessing the power of AI: Japanese delivery firms, restaurants look to tech to boost businesses.* The Japan Times. https://www.japantimes.co.jp/news/2020/02/26/business/tech/ai-solves-problems/#.Xl0pW0MkqRt.

Van Volkenburgh, B. (2019, September 11). *Artificial intelligence and taxes: 8 ways it's being used.* CrowdReason. https://www.crowdreason.com/blog/artificial-intelligence-tax.

Vordenbaeumen, H. (2019, April 24). *3 ways accountants can implement AI today.* Accounting Today https://www.accountingtoday.com/opinion/3-ways-accountants-can-implement-ai-today.

World Economic Forum (2020). *Transforming paradigms: A global AI in financial services survey.* http://www3.weforum.org/docs/WEF_AI_in_Financial_Services_Survey.pdf.

3 Robotic Process Automation (RPA) and AI

Overview of RPA

Organizations of all types and sizes can automate business processes by utilizing RPA software. Many RPA vendors offer automation solutions that do not require its users to have any programming skills; instead, they rely on users activating the robot to mimic keystrokes using a smart screen recording. Unsurprisingly, RPA adoption has grown substantially in recent years. Gartner notes that "robotic process automation has democratized integration and automation, leading to widespread business adoption" (Stoudt-Hansen et al., 2019). Adoption will continue to grow as organizations seek to realize productivity gains, increased accuracy, and cost savings through automation.

According to researchers van der Aalst et al. (2018), there are two characteristics of RPA that have contributed to its growth. First, RPA can layer on top of existing systems, enabling organizations to avoid redesigning or acquiring new platforms. Second, RPA software robots are flexible and can adapt to changes in the underlying information system. These two features of RPA imply that the investment can be relatively small compared to other IT projects. Consequently, RPA is currently viewed as a quick way to increase a firm's return on investment (van der Aalst, Bichler, & Heinzl, 2018).

The automation of accounting processes has the potential to enhance the bottom line. By 2024, Gartner predicts that organizations can lower operational costs by 30% through redesigned operational processes and **hyper-automation, combining** RPA tools and machine learning applications (Stoudt-Hansen et al., 2019).

We defined RPA in Chapter 1 as a software application (commonly referred to as robots or bots) that automates a business process by replicating the actions of humans performing tasks, such as manipulating or transferring data within digital systems. RPA robots automate repetitive tasks, like macros in Excel, helping organizations get more work done in less time. However, a distinguishing feature of an RPA robot is the ability to interface with multiple applications and across functions. PwC describes RPA as "technology agnostic," meaning that it can work across legacy ERPs, mainframes, desktop applications, and any other IT platform (PwC, 2017). In other words, unlike Excel macros, any technology platform that a human can use can also be navigated by an RPA robot.

Additionally, there is some debate over whether RPA should be considered a form of AI. A joint report by CPA Canada and the AICPA notes that RPA by itself does not constitute AI because it performs actions using pre-programmed instructions (CPA Canada & AICPA, 2019). The bots make no additional decisions, and no learning occurs after completing the tasks. Gartner seems to agree with this assessment, describing AI, ML, NLP as "not part of RPA per se, but are closely related" (Miers, Tornbohm, Kerremans, & Ray, 2019). We define AI broadly as a computer program or software application that can imitate or simulate human behavior. As such, RPA's ability to mimic human actions places it on a spectrum where it could be considered an elementary form of AI. UiPath, one of the leading RPA vendors, notes that "RPA robots utilize the user interface to capture data and manipulate applications just like humans do" (UiPath, n.d.).

Whether or not RPA is technically classified as AI is a matter of interpretation. What matters is that RPA is being used extensively in the accounting profession, often coupled with AI and ML technologies. Thus, accountants need to understand what RPA is and how it can be combined with AI.

RPA Vendors

There are currently many RPA solutions on the market. In a 2019 study, Gartner evaluated leading RPA providers based on the features of their solution, including integration via the user interface, large-scale data migration, and augmenting knowledge of workers (Miers et al., 2019). Examples of RPA solutions reviewed in the Gartner study included UiPath, Automation Anywhere, Blue Prism, Kofax, and WorkFusion.

When to Use RPA?

It is essential to consider when it is appropriate to use RPA before its implementation. According to a paper published in the *Journal of*

Emerging Technologies in Accounting, the implementation of RPA is appropriate when: (1) existing processes are well defined; (2) tasks are high volume and repeatable; and (3) tasks are mature, having predictable outcomes and known costs (Moffitt, Rozario, & Vasarhelyi, 2018). Gartner recommends that RPA automate business processes that are predictable and rules-based manual tasks that are well understood (Miers et al., 2019). Deloitte advises using RPA for operations that require manual intervention, are rules-based, and require a significant amount of time (Deloitte, 2017). These recommendations serve as a sound basis for accountants to use when trying to assess whether RPA will provide the desired benefits.

Gartner identified two deployment models for RPA platforms: (1) attended robots that augment human operators, and (2) unattended robots that have a separate and dedicated environment from all humans triggered by remote schedules or activity (e.g., through an API, or some observable event, such as the creation of a file in a directory or the arrival of an email into an account monitored by the robot (Miers et al., 2019).

Another study by Gartner focused primarily on the application of RPA in finance and accounting. It is recommended that RPA is applied for three use cases: (1) transferring data into or between AIS or ERP systems, (2) combining data into standardized reports, and (3) automating an existing structured business process or creating a business process (Tornbohm & Leiter, 2019).

Deloitte provides numerous examples such as transferring data, opening emails and attachments, connecting to system APIs, extracting data from structured documents such as invoices, logging into enterprise applications, performing calculations, collecting social media statistics, scraping data from the web, completing forms, and reading and writing to databases (Deloitte, n.d.).

Advantages and Challenges of RPA

There are several vital functional advantages of using RPA to automate accounting processes. Whereas traditional workflow automation tools rely on application programming interfaces (APIs), RPA robots replicate human activity by observing the user complete a task through a **graphical user interface (GUI)**. In other words, a script is generated through a screen recording of mouse and keyboard actions while completing a task. For example, opening an email and downloading a file to a specific location in the network storage would be a straightforward process to automate. Since building a bot typically requires little or no-coding expertise, it is unnecessary to have a computer science background to build robots.

RPA robots are a digital workforce that can work 24 hours a day, seven days a week. The bots can complete tasks with higher speed and accuracy over a more extended period than humans. As the volume of activity increases, automation through robots can proportionally increase in scale (Costa, 2020). Humans, however,are limited by the physiological need for rest, food, and sleep.

Additionally, RPA facilities regulate compliance, as every action a bot takes is logged and scripted based on rules (Costa, 2020). In this way, RPA helps manage risk, as there are fewer workers that need to access sensitive information that could potentially expose data (Costa, 2020).

There are financial benefits to using RPA as well. As previously mentioned, RPA is easily layered on top of existing information systems and therefore offers the potential for quick wins with little investment (van der Aalst et al., 2018). PwC describes this process as "non-intrusive," meaning that RPA uses the existing interface and does not require costly integration (PwC, 2017). Not requiring integration allows RPA programs to be launched in days or weeks, resulting in a lower cost of implementation.

A strong return on investment (ROI) over many years is also possible. Although the initial costs for RPA licensing and development are high, the rate of return improves significantly past the first year as maintenance costs are less expensive than the development costs. Furthermore, RPA robots can be expected to last for an average of six to eight years (Costa, 2020). Consequently, the more processes that RPA automates, the better the ROI, as the fixed costs are spread over multiple projects (Costa, 2020).

From a user perspective, RPA can involve a wide range of developers, including business analysis and end-users, departmental developers, and enterprise IT professionals (Miers et al., 2019). Further, RPA can be scaled as staff can be trained to maintain, program, and deploy robots (PwC, 2017). As a result, teams and robots can work side by side to increase performance.

Challenges of RPA

Despite the many advantages discussed above, accounting leaders should exercise caution before purchasing an RPA system. It is critical that companies fully understand the limitations of RPA to minimize the effort and money spent on failed initiatives. Gartner, Inc. estimates that 40% of businesses experience buyer's remorse after implementing RPA projects (Tornbohm & Leiter, 2019).

The main challenges of RPA can be grouped into the following three categories: technical, compliance, and process.

A primary technical challenge of RPA bots, especially those without AI capabilities, is that they will fail if they encounter a condition that was not pre-programmed. Thus, RPA agents could make mistakes because of contextual changes (van der Aalst et al., 2018). Similarly, RPA bots are likely to fail if they are fed incorrect or incomplete data, and improper bot design could affect the IT infrastructure (Deloitte, 2018). Other technical challenges include choosing a solution that requires intensive programming or does not demonstrate scalability (AI Multiple, 2020).

Compliance with laws and regulations is another challenge, as automation errors can reduce the accuracy of regulatory reports and expose organizations to fines, sanctions, and legal violations (Deloitte, 2018). Maintaining confidentiality of sensitive information (e.g., social security numbers, compensation, addresses, etc.) is another concern when using RPA. Accounting firms that adopt RPA must ensure that controls are in place to prevent cybersecurity breaches (Moffitt et al., 2018). All RPA automation activity should be logged and audited to ensure proper governance and to mitigate potential compliance issues.

Finally, it is crucial to recognize that RPA cannot improve a process that is already broken. Applying RPA to a broken process only exacerbates the problem, thereby creating errors at a faster rate (Arraya, 2019). Even if the manual process is not broken, applying a poorly designed automation solution can harm operations due to increased processing errors (Deloitte, 2018). Other process challenges include choosing a process that is too complex, changes frequently, or will have a significant business impact (AI Multiple, 2020).

Notwithstanding these challenges, the potential to automate accounting functions and business processes will drive increased demand for RPA in public accounting and industry for years to come.

Applications of RPA in Public Accounting

RPA in Audits

Due to the repetitive nature of many audit tasks, RPA can make financial statement audits more efficient, accurate, and less expensive. A paper in the *Journal of Emerging Technologies in Accounting* comprehensively examines how RPA can be used in audit (Moffitt et al., 2018).

These researchers note that auditors had used various automation tools before RPA became as popular as it is today. For example, Excel macros, IDEA, ACL, R, and Python could all be used to automate various audit tasks. However, many of these tools cannot perform as seamlessly as RPA and may require the user to have basic to advanced programming skills.

For example, auditors use Excel for sample selection, testing, and documenting audit procedures. The audit templates require manual editing to enter data, perform calculations, and document results. Macros can be used to automate certain rules-based functions such as account reconciliations.

Programs such as ACL and IDEA can be used for a variety of audit calculations and use for analytical procedures, internal control testing, and detail testing.

Scriptable languages such as Python and R also facilitate automation but requires users to have strong programming skills. These tools are free and more flexible than Excel, ACL, or IDEA to automate audit tasks.

Although these traditional audit tools are useful, RPA technology can often perform similar tasks more efficiently. As a result, audit firms are increasingly adopting RPA for manual and repetitive audit tasks such as account reconciliations, internal control testing, and detail testing. Popular RPA vendors include UiPath, Blue Prism, and Automation Anywhere. These programs offer similar automation capabilities as Excel, ACL, IDEA, Python, and R but do not require programming at the user-level interface.

As a result, RPA will transform the role of the auditor. Instead of collecting data, processing, analyzing, and disseminating, auditors will focus more on the evaluation component of audit procedures (Moffitt et al., 2018).

Finally, Moffit et al. (2018) note that before this transition takes place, audit firms must consider the following:

1   Which audit process should be targeted for automation?
2   How can audit procedures be distilled into small steps suitable for automation?
3   What audit procedures can result in automation?
4   Are data in a machine-readable format?
5   Based on the assessments made in previous stages, what audit procedures should be targeted for automation?
6   Does RPA function as envisioned in the prototyping stage?
7   Through evaluation and feedback, can areas for improvement be identified? (p. 5)

Valuable insight from these recommendations is vital for firms to develop a framework to assess how RPA can be used strategically in an audit. Firms should target processes that will yield the most significant benefit for the least cost and effort. Carefully thinking about these considerations before implementation, and then monitoring the results after deployment will ensure success.

RPA in Tax

Manual and repetitive tasks commonplace in tax departments are ideal candidates for automation in general and RPA. PwC provides several examples of how RPA can be used for tax functions (PwC, 2017). RPA can export trial balances from ERP systems that will then be used to prepare the tax return. Trial balance information can be converted to a tax basis by assigning book basis accounts to tax basis account numbers and reconciling intercompany transactions. RPA could then assist in preparing the tax returns by automatically completing tax return line items and information fields and then submitting online. Next, RPA could be used to account for taxes by calculating deferred taxes and booking deferred tax accounting entries in the GL system. Finally, RPA could be used to address tax inquiries, such as gathering data to respond to an audit. Fixed asset sub-ledger data, as well as industry and company-specific data, could also be automatically exported.

PwC deployed RPA for one of their consumer healthcare clients, a company with over 100 legal entities with offices worldwide, and in multiple US states (PwC, 2017). This client used a variety of financial systems, trial balances, and chart of accounts. Manual spreadsheets were also used to calculate the interim provision calculations. Due to disparate financial systems and processes, gathering and reconciling the data was a manual and time-consuming process.

PwC's solution was to deploy RPA to ease the following operations: extract the financial information from the ERP systems, clean the data and reconcile accounts, organize the data by a legal entity versus management reporting, analyze account changes (such as accrual book and tax adjustments), and then flag account differences for follow-up investigation. The impact of this intervention accelerated the completion of the income tax provision, reduced manual effort by 10% to 25%, improved overall accuracy, and reduced the time necessary to perform low-value work such as data extraction and manipulation.

Applications of RPA in Corporate Accounting

RPA has been applied to a variety of use cases in corporate accounting. A Gartner study found that RPA can save 25,000 hours of avoidable rework in accounting departments at $878,000 for an organization with 40 full-time accounting staff (Lavelle, 2019). This study involved more than 150 corporate controllers, chief accounting officers, and chief accounting leaders in determining the main benefits of RPA. However, the same survey found that only 29% of RPA adopters have implemented technology for financial reporting purposes. Thus, there is a significant opportunity for accounting and finance departments to leverage RPA to make financial reporting more efficient, accurate, and less costly. Processes that are well defined, rules-based, high volume, predictable, and repeatable are ideal for automating.

Eline Oh, ACMA, CGMA, CPA (Australia) implemented RPA for cash management at an investment firm by hiring contractors who customized the RPA implementation. After implementation, employees no longer had to fund investment bank accounts manually or to move funds between inter-company accounts (O'Neill, 2020).

Gartner features a Fortune 500 multinational company that hired the consulting firm WonderBotz as a case study (Tornbohm & Leiter, 2019). WonderBotz built a customized reconciliation tool called ReconBotz using Blue Prism's RPA platform for the general ledger reconciliation process, which was highly manual. By using ReconBotz, it automated 95% of its 5,000 reconciliations per month. Typically, it would take an accountant 30 minutes to complete one reconciliation, for a total of 150,000 minutes or 2,500 hours. After implementing RPA (ReconBotz), this process was reduced to three hours to complete all the reconciliations.

Implementation of RPA

The abundance of RPA software providers combined with the relative ease of building robots to automate simple processes might cause accountants to underestimate what it takes to implement RPA for more involved initiatives effectively. As Gartner states, "once organizations move beyond simple examples, there is a critical need [sic] for multi-disciplinary governance and coordination across business units, IT, security, sourcing and assurance functions. Without this comprehensive approach, many organizations experience buyer's remorse due to poor ROI, misaligned resources, siloed usage, and inability to scale."

(Stoudt-Hansen et al., 2019). Thus, accountants must consider the proper circumstances under which to implement RPA carefully.

A *Financial Management* article recommends considering the following three key areas before introducing RPA (O'Neill, 2020): select a process, clearly define the scope, and get buy-in from staff.

Selecting a process refers to management being incredibly careful with the initial project selection. As stated in the O'Neill 2020 article, one school of thought is to experiment with a process to get a "proof of concept" to demonstrate how it works and ensure staff is used to the idea of RPA. The problem with this approach is that they are unlikely to yield a meaningful return on investment. A second approach is to document and measure existing processes using key performance indicators. After evaluation of the results, select the process to automate.

Clearly defining the scope refers to management setting reasonable expectations regarding RPA capabilities. By doing so, staff will be more likely to have a balanced assessment of the results of automation and less likely to focus on the failures of RPA. As Rand Low, a senior fellow at the University of Queensland's Business School in Australia, states, "Humans are reluctant to trust an automated system and will focus on the rare moments where the RPA fails rather than on when it succeeds" (O'Neill, 2020).

Getting buy-in from staff recognizes that employees may be reluctant to embrace RPA for fear of being replaced by robots and losing their jobs. Reassuring employees entails communicating that RPA will upskill staff and keep them on the forefront of industry developments. Reassurance requires investments in teaching staff how RPA works and training on how to use it.

> To shift perceptions, managers and employees need to talk about how responsibilities and processes will change, what training will be available, and if professional development can be pursued in place of manual tasks that will be removed from a team's workweek.
>
> (O'Neill, 2020, para. 15)

Gartner provides three additional recommendations to consider that are more technical: (1) explore the relative advantages of various RPA products by distinguishing between the needs of the developers and those required for sufficient scale across the organization; (2) optimize the likelihood by defining the corporate use cases and the capabilities essential to the business and aligning them to strategic objectives in the long term; and (3) maximize ROI by prioritizing and selecting an RPA product that has broad functional capabilities to support the primary core functions of the business, while also paying close attention to tangential capabilities, such as AI and ML (Miers et al., 2019). This type of analysis ideally is performed by a team of accounting, finance, IT, and strategic management personnel working together.

Why RPA Fails

Despite the increasing adoption of RPA across industries, the mistakes that many organizations make during implementation have resulted in a 30% to 50% failure rate on initial projects (EY, 2016). According to EY (2016), the top 10 common issues for failed RPA projects are:

1 Not considering RPA as business-led, as opposed to IT-led
2 Not having an RPA business case and postponing planning until after proofs-of-concept (POCs) or pilots
3 Underestimating what happens after processes have been automated
4 Treating Robotics as a series of automation versus an end-to-end change program
5 Targeting RPA at the wrong processes
6 Applying traditional delivery methodologies
7 Automating too much of a process or not optimizing for RPA
8 Forgetting about IT infrastructure
9 Assuming RPA alone is sufficient to achieve an excellent ROI
10 Assuming the skills needed to create a POC are good enough for production automation. (pp. 4–10)

The most complicated issue to deal with when it comes to RPA failures relates to the people, not the technology. The first consideration noted by EY speaks to the importance of management involved with an automation project. Deploying robots will result in a virtual workforce across the entire organization: Consequently, business leaders, not IT specialists, should be responsible for prioritizing which processes are automated for managing the workforce. The business leaders should collaborate with IT, Cyber, Security, Risk Management, and others.

Another implementation challenge is pursuing RPA development with in-house teams that do not have sufficient training or capacity (AI Multiple, 2020).

Integrating RPA with AI/ML Applications

Van der Aalst et al. (2018) suggests that RPA must become smarter through integration with AI and ML techniques for adoption to become more pervasive. The more RPA can be integrated with AI and ML applications, the more significant the potential impact on the accounting profession. Gartner ranks the most common ways in which AI/ML is implemented in RPA products, categorized by use: (1) RPA paired with computer vision algorithms, (2) optical character recognition to read and interpret the text; (3) automated business process and task discovery, (4) augmented content analytics, and (5) NLP and natural language generation (NLG) (Miers et al., 2019). All these integrated implementations could provide substantial benefits to the accounting profession going forward.

References

AI Multiple. (2020, June 4). *20 RPA pitfalls & the checklist for avoiding them [2020 update]*. https://blog.aimultiple.com/rpa-pitfalls/.

Arraya. (2019, January 9). *5 RPA mistakes businesses keep making (and how to get it right)*. https://www.arrayasolutions.com/5-rpa-mistakes-businesses-keep-making-and-how-to-get-it-right/.

Costa, A. M. (2020). Robotic process automation: Bringing on bots to enhance a CPA's work. *Pennsylvania CPA Journal, 90*(4), 28–30.

CPA Canada, & AICPA. (2019). *A CPA's introduction to AI: From algorithms to deep learning.* CPA Canada. https://www.cpacanada.ca/en/business-and-accounting-resources/other-general-business-topics/information-management-and-technology/publications/a-cpa-introduction-to-ai.

Deloitte. (n.d.). *Tax value of robotic process automation (RPA): Understanding tax RPA use cases.* https://www2.deloitte.com/us/en/pages/tax/solutions/tax-robotic-process-automation.html.

Deloitte. (2017). *Robotic process automation – What does robotic process automation really offer, and how should you be thinking about it.* https://www2.deloitte.com/content/dam/Deloitte/us/Documents/process-and-operations/us-sdt-connections-robotic.pdf.

Deloitte. (2018, February 7). *Finance and accounting robotic process automation a priority as over half plan to improve digital controllership in 2018.* https://www2.deloitte.com/us/en/pages/about-deloitte/articles/press-releases/finance-accounting-robotic-process-automation-priority-for-digital-controllership-2018-deloitte.html.

EY. (2016). *Get ready for robots: Why planning makes the difference between success and disappointment.* https://www.ey.com/Publication/vwLUAssets/Get_ready_for_robots/$FILE/ey-get-ready-for-robots.pdf.

Lavelle, J. (2019, October 2). *Gartner says robotic process automation can save finance departments 25,000 hours of avoidable work annually.* Gartner. https://www.gartner.com/en/newsroom/press-releases/2019-10-02-gartner-says-robotic-process-automation-can-save-fina.

Miers, D., Tornbohm, C., Kerremans, M., & Ray, S. (2019, December 3). *Critical capabilities for robotic process automation* (ID: G00385052). Retrieved from Gartner Database.

Moffitt, K. C., Rozario, A. M., & Vasarhelyi, M. A. (2018). Robotic process automation for auditing. *Journal of Emerging Technologies in Accounting,* *15*(1), 1–10. https://doi.org/10.2308/jeta-10589.

O'Neill, L. (2020). 3 tips for introducing RPA. *Financial Management.* https://www.fm-magazine.com/news/2020/feb/robotic-process-automation-rpa-benefits-22587.html.

PwC. (2017, May). *Robotic process automation (RPA): What tax needs to know now.* https://www.pwc.com/gx/en/tax/publications/assets/pwc-tax-function-of-the-future-focus-on-today-robotics-process-automation.pdf.

Stoudt-Hansen, S., Karamouzis, F., Villa, A., Ray, S., Dunie, R., Sturgill, N., Shotton, L., Miers, D., Biscotti, F. (2019, December 10). *Predicts 2020: RPA renaissance driven by morphing offerings and zeal for operational excellence* (ID: G00465015). Retrieved from Gartner Database.

Tornbohm, C., & Leiter, G. (2019, February 19). *When and how to use robotic process automation in finance and accounting* (ID: G00377790). Retrieved from Gartner Database.

UiPath. (n.d.). *Robotic process automation (RPA): The only automation software for today's enterprise.* https://www.uipath.com/rpa/robotic-process-automation.

van der Aalst, W. M. P., Bichler, M., & Heinzl, A. (2018). Robotic process automation. *Business and Information Systems Engineering,* *60*(4), 269–272. https://doi.org/10.1007/s12599-018-0542-4.

4 Text Mining

What is text mining?

In Chapter 1, we introduced the term "text mining" and defined it as follows:

> Text mining is a process of extracting information from various text sources (such as Word documents, PDF files, social media posts, emails, websites, articles, XML files, and others) to discover patterns, trends, and themes. Text found in these documents is typically unstructured, i.e., they are not in a predefined format that can be analyzed through data analytics software such as IDEA or ACL. Text mining is performed in two steps: (1) imposing structure on the text data sources, and then (2) using data mining techniques to extract relevant information.
>
> (Sharda et al., 2014)

There are multiple definitions of text mining in the literature. A critical preliminary point to make is that that text mining goes beyond information retrieval.

The purpose of information retrieval is to differentiate between relevant and non-relevant texts, with the primary goal to enable information access or make it faster and more accurate. The purpose of text mining is to analyze texts and uncover new insights from them, with a primary goal to gain new actionable knowledge or to improve decision-making.

In other words, text mining is a form of data mining that analyzes patterns from *unstructured* text sources as opposed to *structured* sources, such as databases.

Early research on text mining refers to it as the process of knowledge discovery from extensive collections of unstructured textual data

(Feldman & Dagan, 1995). In her essay on text mining (Hearst, 2003), Professor Marti Hearst of the University of California, Berkeley defines text mining as the computer-led discovery of new, previously unknown information by automatically extracting information from different written resources. She adds that "a key element is the linking together of the extracted information together to form new facts or new hypotheses to be explored further by more conventional means of experimentation". In line with that stream of research, Professor Catherine Blake of the University of Illinois at Urbana-Champaign characterizes text mining as the process of identifying novel, interesting, and understandable patterns from a collection of texts (Blake, 2011, p. 126). For professor Stephane Tuffery of the University of Rennes in France, text mining is the set of techniques and methods used for the automatic processing of natural language text data available in reasonably large quantities in the form of computer files, to extract and structure their contents and themes, for rapid (non-literary) analysis, the discovery of hidden data, or automatic decision making (Tuffery, 2011, p. 627).

Text mining is also referred to as text analytics. These terms are often used interchangeably in the literature and practice. However, there is a subtle difference between the two words: Text analytics may be viewed as more focused on the visualization aspects (graphs, reports), using the results from analyses processed by text mining. However, for this book, we use these terms interchangeably.

Text Mining has gained tremendous momentum recently mainly because of the exponential growth of content on the internet with web-enabled applications and social networks, most of which contain unstructured text. Text Mining has also grown because of the rapid digitalization of business processes as organizations moved away from paper to electronic documents and other digital records. Finally, the significant technological advances in cloud computing, AI, the internet of things (IoT), and big data analytics have had a notable impact on the amount of data available for text mining.

The role of natural language processing in text mining

Text mining, as a process of knowledge discovery from unstructured texts, requires natural language interpretation. For this reason, natural language processing (NLP), which is the process by which a computer program interprets natural language like speech or text, is one of the most important concepts and methodologies for enabling text mining to extract actionable knowledge effectively and efficiently from texts.

As defined in Chapter 1, NLP is a subfield of AI that focuses on the interaction of computers and people using human languages. This subfield can be broken down further into two types: natural language understanding and natural language generation.

As we will discuss in this chapter, NLP techniques involve both statistical and machine learning approaches.

Overview of Text Mining Research

Text mining is a multidisciplinary branch of knowledge that involves concepts and techniques from such disparate fields as the library and information sciences, linguistics, computer sciences, and data sciences (i.e., statistics and data mining). These text mining techniques are applied and used in numerous domains, such as in medical research, bibliometric studies, marketing, government, political research, and technology.

Considerable research has been published in the field of text mining in many of these domains. A study of the text mining literature published under the subject category "Information Science Library Science" in the Web of Science Database during 1999–2013 counted more than 36,000 text mining-related research papers, with research contributions in various subjects such as biology, technology, chemistry, physics, medical sciences, and the social sciences (Nagarkar & Kumbhar, 2015).

In the financial sector, abundant literature exists documenting the application of data mining in areas such as stock market predictions, financial risk analysis, and fraud detection. In contrast, text mining in financial applications has emerged only recently (Pejic-Bach et al., 2019). This new development of text mining in the financial sector has allowed researchers and organizations to identify new valuable patterns and insights from unstructured text sources such as corporate documents, social media posts, emails, and call logs. Most of this emerging research is primarily focused on external data sources, such as news and online media posts, for stock market predictions and fraud detections. The number of research studies using internal data sources is still relatively low (Pejic-Bach et al., 2019).

A 2016 survey of the applications of text mining in the financial domain (Kumar & Ravi, 2016) categorized the emerging literature in the following areas:

- Foreign exchange (FOREX) rate prediction: e.g., mining of news for exchange rate forecasting;
- Stock market prediction: e.g., mining of financial news and textual information available on websites for financial market predictions or stock price prediction;
- Customer relationship management: e.g., mining of customer reviews, complaints, news or social media contents for customer opinion or sentiment analysis; and
- Cybersecurity, fraud, and other risk detection: e.g., anomaly detection in email systems, spam, phishing, and malware detection, churn prediction, bankruptcy prediction, financial statement fraud.

However, more investigations remain to be done to advance text mining research in these areas as well as in new financial application areas.

A 2019 study (Lewis & Young, 2019) reviewed papers employing textual analysis methods published in leading accounting and finance journals over the period 2010-2018. Lewis and Young found the accounting and finance profession has been slow to adopt mainstream natural language processing (NLP) methods. Instead, accounting and finance professionals preferred simple approaches such as keyword searches, word counts, and dictionaries that measure specific attributes such as tone and readability scores. The study also highlights the small but growing body of work applying specific NLP techniques, including machine learning classifiers and statistical methods for identifying topic structure, at the document or corpus level. Finally, the authors discuss the opportunities and challenges to improving NLP usage in financial reporting research moving forward, pointing access to text resources and interdisciplinary and intersectoral collaboration among the main impediments to future progress.

In summary, the use of text mining in the finance and accounting literature is still a new trend. Future growth in adoption will be driven by:

- Improvements in data access,
- Increased collaboration among researchers from various disciplines and between academia and practice, and
- The growing availability of resources in big data analytics, machine learning, and artificial intelligence.

Methods and Technologies Used in Text Mining

Text mining systems consist of a wide range of techniques and algorithms (computer programs) that are generally found in libraries of programming languages (e.g., Python, R) or in software applications for text mining (e.g., SAS Text Miner, IBM Watson NLU).

The market for text mining applications is highly fragmented. A 2018 study from Gartner provided 39 of the most visible text analytics vendors (Davis et al., 2018). Examples of vendors listed in the Gartner report include SAS (Text Miner), IBM (Watson and SPSS Text Analytics for Surveys), Google (Cloud Natural Language API), Amazon (Amazon Comprehend), Microsoft Azure (Text Analytics), Expert system (Cogito), Lexalytics (Lexalytics Intelligence Platform), OpenText (OpenText Content Analytics, OpenText Sentiment), SAP (SAP HANA Text Mining XS classic), and Verint Systems (Text Analytics).

Reusing the classification proposed by researchers Martin Rajman and Martin Vesely of the Laboratory of Artificial Intelligence of the Swiss Federal Institute of Technology (Rajman and Vesely, 2004), we can classify text mining techniques and algorithms into one of three categories: document preprocessing, mining (or, data mining for textual data), and visualization.

* **Document preprocessing** includes the following subcategories: data selection and filtering, data cleaning, document representation, morphological normalization, and parsing, and semantic analysis;
* **Mining** (data mining for textual data) includes clustering, classification, entity, and relation extraction; and
* **Visualization** includes visualization techniques for multidimensional data and text summarization.

In the following subsections, we summarize the text mining techniques and algorithms used in each category and subcategory.

Document Preprocessing

Data Selection and Filtering

Data selection and filtering techniques and algorithms are used to reduce the texts to their most relevant items for analysis or action. More specifically, data selection assists users with the identification and retrieval of related documents based on the explicit descriptive metadata with which they are associated, such as keywords or descriptors. Data filtering then evaluates the documents' relevance based on their actual content using relevance measures.

Data Cleaning

Data cleaning tools are used to remove noise such as spelling errors, inconsistencies, and unnecessary items from the textual data, and to identify metalinguistic information. These tools assist users in:

- Correcting mistakes,
- Normalizing text (e.g., letter case normalization, abbreviation normalization),
- Removing parts that are not part of the processed language,
- Removing stop words (i.e., unnecessary words), punctuations, and special characters, and
- Assigning metalinguistic tags to words. Metalinguistic tags include:
  - o **Named entity recognition (NER)**, a type of algorithm that identifies relevant nouns of named entities such as people, places, organizations, or dates, and
  - o **Part-of-speech (POS) tagging**, a type of algorithm that assigns to each word an identifier, such as noun, verb, adjective, and others.

Document Representation

Document representation algorithms transform unstructured text into a representation that the system can interpret for analysis or visualization. A simple representation approach is the bag-of-words (BoW) approach, where a text such as a document or a sentence is represented as a string of words, disregarding their order in the text and grammar. A popular BoW representation often used for text documents is the vector space model (VSM). In a VSM, each text document is represented as a vector, and the vector space is represented by the words in the text document with their respective importance (weight), measured in terms of frequency of occurrence (i.e., the number of times the word appears in the text document).

More complex representation models include more structured semantic models.

Keikha et al. (2008) distinguish four different types of document representation: N-grams, single terms, phrases, and a logic-based document representation called rich document representation (RDR).

1   The N-gram representation is a string-based representation with no linguistic processing. It is the simplest representation, where documents are represented as strings of n words.

2   The single-term approach is based on words with minimum linguistic processing. In this approach, documents are represented as vectors of their distinct words and their importance as described earlier (Vector Space Model approach). Most often, the stem (i.e., root) of the words is used instead of the words themselves to increase document matching results.

3   The phrase approach is based on linguistically formed phrases and single words. It is a more sophisticated approach that involves extracting statistical or linguistic phrases and representing documents with their stemmed single words and phrases.

4   The rich document representation (RDR) provides a more semantic representation of a document. It is based on linguistic processing (such as part-of-speech tagging and matching rules) and represents documents as a set of logical terms and statements that describe the relationships in the text. For example, a proposition such as "for" in the sentence fragment "....operating systems for personal computers..." suggests a relationship between "operating systems" and "personal computers" (Keikha et al., 2008).

There are also document representation models that are based on concepts (rather than on words alone). In a concept-based representation, a document is represented as a vector of concepts. The importance of the concepts is measured in terms of frequency of occurrence. A hierarchical or lattice structure represents the number of times the concept appears in the document as a hierarchical "is-a" relation. For example, if a document contains the three related concepts, "cat," "dog," and "animal," "animal" would be a super-class of both "cat" and "dog" (Da Costa Pereira & Tettamanzi, 2006).

The more sophisticated approaches above allow greater understanding of the meaning of the texts by the software and enable systems to produce more accurate and useful results in terms of information retrieval, analysis, and visualization.

Morphological Normalization and Parsing

Morphological normalization refers to natural language tasks such as stemming, lemmatization (i.e., reduction of words to their stems), and part-of-speech tagging, as described earlier (see Data Cleaning subsection above).

Parsing refers to the process of assigning syntactic structure to the normalized text, including text segmentation, sentence chunking into smaller syntactic units such as phrases, and the identification of syntactic relations between the identified units (Rajman & Vesely, 2004).

Semantic Analysis

Semantic analysis tools resolve semantic ambiguities. These tools use techniques such as word sense disambiguation (WSD), anaphora resolution, and co-reference resolution. The semantic analysis also assesses topical proximity among and within the documents. These tools further increase the system's ability to interpret the meaning of texts.

A representative (non-exhaustive) list of these techniques and algorithms is summarized below:

- **Word sense disambiguation (WSD)** enables systems to interpret words that have multiple meanings (i.e., word senses), depending on the context. WSD tools use context to assign the appropriate meaning to a word, determined by the other words around that word in the text.
- **Anaphora resolution** tools assist in resolving what pronouns (e.g., they, he, she, it) or noun phrases refer to in a text. (Note: a noun phrase is a noun with a modifier that modifies that noun. For example: in the following noun phrases "his cat," "Paul's cat," and "the grey cat," "cat" is the noun, and "his," "Paul's," and "the grey" are modifiers).
- **Co-reference** tools assist in finding expressions that refer to the same entity. Co-reference occurs when two mentions refer to the same entity, such as in "She taught herself," "She," and "herself" refer to the same person (Random House Kernerman Webster., n.d.).
- **Latent semantic analysis (LSA)** refers to techniques and algorithms that assist in uncovering synonyms, homonyms, and term dependencies, such as pairs or groups of words.
- Another type of semantic models and algorithms is the **latent Dirichlet allocation (LDA)**, which refers to techniques and systems that identify topics from the words of a collection of documents, representing a document as a mixture of topics (and a topic as a mixture of words). Latent Dirichlet allocation (LDA) is a popular topic modeling technique in natural language processing.
- Measures used to assess topical proximity include vector space similarity measures such as the generalized Euclidean distance,

cosine similarity, and Chi-square distance, and other measures such as measures based on phrase occurrence, measures based on the length of the document under evaluation, and the average document length in the whole collection, and others (Rajman & Vesely, 2004).

Semantic analysis is a particularly challenging area in natural language processing, and it is evolving rapidly. This includes applying machine learning approaches to these methodologies, which further improves the software's ability to interpret natural language.

Mining

Clustering

Document clustering is a machine learning technique that groups documents into clusters based on their similarity. For text mining, clustering is used for various functions such as document selection, organization, summarization, and visualization.

There are multiple approaches to clustering, and a wide variety of algorithms exist for completing this task.

Clustering algorithms are typically unsupervised (refer to our definition of unsupervised learning in Chapter 1).

The most well-known clustering algorithm is the "k-means" algorithm. In this algorithm, each cluster is represented by the mean of all its closest data points (i.e., each cluster representing a cluster of documents grouped by the algorithm based on their similarity measure or distance measure). Similar clustering techniques use other measures of central tendencies, such as the median or the mode. Different clustering methodologies include density-based clustering and hierarchical clustering.

Classification

Document classification is a machine learning technique that assigns predefined classes to documents.

In contrast to clustering algorithms, classification algorithms are typically supervised. Researchers provide the algorithm with training examples that include the correct class (also called classification or category) and the features used to represent each document (such as the vector-based representation). The classification algorithm then constructs a model that best maps the given features to each class.

When the training data have only two classes, a binary classifier is constructed. Where there are more than two classes, a multi-class classifier is required (Blake, 2011).

Examples of classification algorithms include:

- k-nearest neighbors (based on proximity to the k closest training example),
- Naïve Bayes (probabilistic model based on Bayes' theorem of conditional probability),
- Support vector machines (models where training data is represented as points in space separated into categories),
- Decision trees (based on a top-down tree structure with "if-then" rules learned from the training data) and other decision rules-based models, and
- Neural networks (models that emulate the way the human brain processes information).

There are several applications of document classification, such as spam filtering, email routing, content tagging (which improves browsing and accelerates searches in extensive unstructured text collections), and customer opinion and sentiment analysis.

Entity and Relation Extraction

Entity extraction algorithms are used to extract entities such as person names, organization names, locations, dates, phone numbers, reference numbers, prices, amounts, and other items, from documents.

Relation extraction algorithms are used to identify and characterize relations between entities such as person-organization (e.g., an employee of), person-location (e.g., born in), or organization-location (e.g., headquartered in). Some algorithms focus on event extraction, which is aimed at identifying entities that are related to an event.

Information extraction (IE) algorithms use various machine learning approaches, including rule learning-based methods, classification-based methods, and sequential labeling-based methods (Tang et al., 2008).

- **Rule learning-based systems** use predefined instructions on extracting the desired information (i.e., words or text fragments) from the text. They include:

- o **Dictionary-based systems**: these systems first construct a pattern (template) dictionary, and then use the dictionary to extract the needed information from text.
- o **Rule-based systems**: these systems use general rules instead of a dictionary to extract information from text.
- o **Wrapper systems**: a wrapper is an extraction procedure consisting of a set of extraction rules and program codes to extract information from certain structured and semi-structured documents such as Web pages.

- **Classification-based systems** cast information extraction as a classification task (i.e., extraction rules are built based on a classification model).
- **Sequential labeling-based extraction systems** cast information extraction as a task of sequential labeling. In sequential labeling, a document is viewed as a sequence of tokens (i.e., words), and a sequence of labels (such as part-of-speech tags). These systems enable describing the dependencies between target information (to be extracted). The dependencies can be utilized to improve the accuracy of the extraction (Tang et al., 2008).

There are multitudes of applications of information extraction from documents in today's digital business environment. Examples include:

- Automated metadata generation for digital libraries,
- Automated information extraction in day-to-day business applications for data entry automation (e.g., information extraction from resumes, receipts, invoices, legal documents, and others),
- Automated information extraction from emails, social media, or other text sources for purposes such as IT security, compliance monitoring, or marketing research,
- Automated document review and analysis for various purposes such as compliance, fraud risk or credit risk detection, audit, financial investigation, scientific research, or patent analysis,
- Product or movie recommender systems based on patterns extracted from purchase orders or social media contents, and
- Automated information extraction from SEC filings and other investor communication materials (e.g., press releases, transcripts of earnings calls) for stock market analysis, firm financial performance or stock price movement predictions, or fraud detection

Visualization

Visualization Techniques for Multidimensional Data

Visualization techniques refer to graphical representations of the data mined from texts. Examples include word clouds, tag clouds, histograms, scatter plots, line plots, box plots, network graphs, and other graphs. Visualization is commonly used for representing text mining analysis results from clustering, topical proximity analysis, sentiment analysis, or other analyses.

Visualization is a critical part of the text mining process, and in data mining in general.

As researcher Daniel Keim (2002) put it:

> Visual data exploration aims at integrating the human in the data exploration process, applying its perceptual abilities to the large data sets available in today's computer systems. The basic idea of visual data exploration is to present the data in some visual form, allowing the human to get insight into the data, draw conclusions, and directly interact with the data.
>
> ... In addition to the direct involvement of the user, the main advantages of visual data exploration over automatic data mining techniques from statistics or machine learning are:
>
> • Visual data exploration can easily deal with highly nonhomogeneous and noisy data,
> • Visual data exploration is intuitive and requires no understanding of complex mathematical or statistical algorithms or parameters.
>
> As a result, visual data exploration usually allows faster data exploration and often provides better results, especially in cases where automatic algorithms fail. (p. 1)

Researcher Daniel Keim (2002) has provided a comprehensive classification of visualization techniques, from simpler to more sophisticated techniques. Simpler methodologies such as 2D/3D displays are suited for small and low-dimensional data sets. Sophisticated techniques, such as geometrically transformed displays, icon-based displays, dense pixel displays, and others, are used for multidimensional, text and hypertext, and other data sets. Interaction and distortion techniques, such as dynamic projections, zooming, filtering, and others, are associated with these visualization methods. Daniel Keim's article (2002) includes illustrations of some of these visualization techniques. Illustrations of information visualization for text mining can also be found in Professor Marti Hearst's book (2009).

Text Summarization

Text summarization consists of a reductive transformation of the source text to summary text through content reduction by selection and generalization of what is important in the source (Sparck-Jones, 1999).

The field of automated text summarization has been the subject of intense research over the past decades. It continues to receive ample attention given that text summarization (like semantic analysis) remains one of the most challenging tasks for computer systems. The growing interest and need for text summarization technologies have been driven by the exponential growth of unstructured texts on the internet and the recent advances in natural language processing and machine learning.

Automated text summarization systems provide many benefits. These include:

- Reducing manual efforts in reading or browsing documents,
- Improving efficiencies and effectiveness in the summarization process,
- Facilitating document selection and indexing,
- Enriching answers in question answering systems, and
- Improving quality and consistency (by eliminating potential human errors or omissions in text summarization using manual efforts).

In addition, automated text summarization has the potential benefit of removing human biases in the summarization process.

Additional considerations regarding automated text summarization are discussed hereafter.

Kumar et al. (2016) distinguish between two types of automatic summarization outputs: extractive or abstractive summaries.

- **Extractive summaries** (or extracts) are produced by identifying meaningful sentences directly selected from the document. Important sentences can be automatically determined using criteria such as word frequency, sentence position, presence of title word, or other criteria, and using a training model (machine learning approach).

- **Abstractive summaries** (or Abstractive summarizations) are produced when the selected document sentences are combined coherently and compressed to exclude unimportant sections of the sentences (Kumar et al., 2016). Building abstractive summaries requires highly sophisticated language modeling and is a more complex task for computer systems than building extractive summaries.

As professor Torres-Moreno pointed out in his book (2014), there are many variants of automatic text summarization. Variants include generic or guided (i.e., personalized), single-document, multi-document, and multilingual summarization, and there are also various combinations of the above. Each task features different challenges that require different approaches to tackle them. Additional variants of automatic text summarization algorithms described by professor Torres-Moreno include domain-specific summarization (e.g., chemistry, biomedical, legal), update summarization (i.e., new facts only), sentence compression and multi-sentence fusion, semantic summarization, and ultra-summarization (summarization of short texts). Professor Torres-Moreno discusses many types of methods and algorithms for text summarization available today, including those involving machine learning approaches, and among them, artificial neural networks.

The use of deep learning in text summarization has gained significant interest recently and is a fertile topic for new research. As discussed in Chapter 1, deep learning is a subset of machine learning that uses artificial neural networks (ANNs) to discover patterns from data, here texts, in the context of text mining. For example, researchers Sukriti Verma and Vagisha Nidhi (2019) proposed an extractive text summarization approach for factual reports using a deep learning model. This model explores various features (e.g., most frequently occurring words, sentence position, sentence length, and others) to improve the set of sentences selected for the summary and the accuracy of the summary.

Zhang et al. (2016) developed a document summarization framework based on a **convolutional neural network (CNN) model**. This framework learns sentence features and performs sentence ranking jointly, using a regression process for sentence ranking and pre-trained word vectors. A **convolutional neural network** is a type of deep neural network initially used for computer vision tasks and more recently used for natural language processing tasks. The use of deep learning approaches has also been explored for abstractive text summarization (Chopra et al., 2016; Nallapati et al., 2016; Rush et al., 2015; Song et al., 2019).

In conclusion, automatic summarization algorithms represent a vibrant and dynamic field of research. These algorithms are continually evolving to improve their performance and to address new challenges. Challenges include the systems' ability to process increasingly large amounts of unstructured texts (blogs, emails, social media posts, and others) and other multimedia contents (images, audio, and video) in global, multilingual environments.

Advantages and Disadvantages of Text Mining

As discussed earlier, text mining is widely used in various industries because it enables users to conduct data mining from large amounts of unstructured texts as opposed to being restricted to structured data from specific databases, such as relational databases. Data mining unstructured text is particularly critical given the recent exponential growth of unstructured text contents on the internet with the expansion of e-commerce, social media, and digital business models across all industries. Indeed, many enterprises have evolved from paper-based to digital transactions, from physical sales and supply chain channels to digital platforms, and from on-premises applications to cloud-based applications.

In this context, more electronic textual data is being generated on the internet every day. Text mining enables users to analyze this vast repository for insights and decision making across all business functions, such as marketing, research, and development, customer service, operations, and supply chain management as well as finance and administrative services.

Hence, text mining is an essential part of data mining, especially in the era of big data. Unstructured textual data (e.g., documents, websites, emails, messages, social media posts, descriptions of audio and video files, transcripts, speech-to-text conversion files, and others) represents the majority of the contents available for data mining in today's digital world.

There are other advantages to text mining. These include:

- It provides significant efficiency gains in the selection, review, and summarization of contents compared to any other alternatives (such as manual or semi-manual processes).

- It enables users to uncover patterns and insights timelier (speed of processing and analysis because of automation).
- It provides insights that humans might not have been able to uncover using traditional methods. (Where conventional research methods are based on samples, text mining can process the entire population of contents).
- It executes its tasks with more consistency compared to human processing, thus presenting the potential to eliminate human errors and human biases.
- Its algorithms enable further automation beyond text mining. For example, text mining outcomes can be integrated into question answering systems. Information extraction algorithms, combined with Optical Character Recognition (OCR) technology, can also be integrated into enterprise systems to automate data entry such as automated contract data entries in an audit or compliance management system, automated resume data entry in a job application system, automated receipt data entry in an employee expense reporting, or automated invoice recording and processing in an accounts payable system.

Text mining also comes with significant disadvantages or limitations. Text mining's main disadvantages are its high complexity and limitations in semantic analysis and abstractive summarization. Considerable progress has been achieved in text mining with AI and machine learning lately, and technologies continue to evolve rapidly.

However, as we draft this book, text mining technologies are still far from matching humans in tasks involving the semantic analysis and abstractive summarization. Besides, tasks such as information extraction require significant human efforts in training the algorithms and reviewing, correcting, and augmenting the outcomes during the processing of documents. The accuracy obtained from automation often requires validation and additional input from humans, requiring a combination of machine and human processing.

Another potential disadvantage of text mining is its lack of transparency or interpretability sometimes. Lack of transparency occurs when the algorithms use black-box approaches, where the internal logic or workings of the algorithms are hidden, making it difficult to explain how the system arrived at a particular outcome or prediction.

Also, the use of text mining requires consideration of privacy and compliance with regulations. For example, using text mining on an individual's emails or social media contents might violate consumer privacy laws or otherwise raise ethical concerns. Information analyzed in text mining might be misused or conducted in a way that is unethical or biased, thus exposing the organization to other risks such as security, copyright infringement, or discrimination risks.

Finally, maintaining text mining algorithms and machine learning training sets can be a daunting task. In rapidly changing environments and highly regulated industries, this problem is magnified by the rapid pace of technology changes, organizational changes, and other factors. Maintaining valid training sets properly is particularly true in the world of accounting, where standards, rules, and regulations are continually changing.

Current and Potential Applications of Text Mining in Accounting

Text mining has made its way to accounting, but its use among accounting professionals is only developing. While the "Big Four" are notable early adopters of these technologies, we are now seeing other accounting organizations starting to adopt or experiment with these technologies as well.

The current and potential applications of text mining technologies in accounting can be summarized in four families of applications: audit automation, accounting automation, tax automation, and business advisory applications.

Audit Automation

Some accounting firms have reported using text mining software for automating contract reviews for audit or compliance assessment. Examples of adoption include Deloitte, EY, and EisnerAmper (Alarcon et al., 2019). Automated contract reviews can be performed as part of organizations' annual financial audits and domain-specific audits such as fraud detection, internal audits, or IT audits. For example, contract reviews for assessing compliance with the latest lease accounting standards has been automated using contract review software such as Kira ("Deloitte Harnesses the Power of Kira for Lease Accounting Contract Review," 2020).

In addition to contract reviews, current or potential applications of text mining in auditing include the review of SEC filings and other corporate communications materials, employment agreements, financing agreements, customer contracts, vendor contracts, and other documentation in support of transactions, financial statements, and disclosures.

In their 2018 article, professors Ting Sun and Miklos Vasarhelyi of Rutgers University stress the importance of textual data in auditing and advocate for the use of deep learning techniques by auditors. Sun and Vasarhelyi also analyze the usefulness of the information provided by various textual data in auditing. Their article provides a guide for auditors to implement deep learning, making the case that deep learning can support audit decision-making in all audit phases, including planning, internal control evaluation, substantive test, and completion (2018).

Accounting Automation

Accounting automation has started to incorporate **intelligent information extraction** (i.e., information extraction using machine learning approaches) in several areas. One of these areas is data entry automation. Indeed, accounting applications have started to embed or integrate information extraction, machine learning software combined with OCR technology and RPA solutions. These applications automatically record transactions (such as accounts payable invoices) and process them, or simply suggest journal entries based on the data extracted, a knowledge base, and patterns learned by the system from the prior transactions.

Similarly, applications of these technologies exist in employee expense reporting, where systems now can leverage OCR technology and intelligent information extraction from receipts to automate data entry and process expense reports.

Text mining applications can also be found in procurement to manage vendor contract compliance. In these cases, text mining can analyze vendor contracts to ensure compliance with policies or improve visibility into procurement patterns.

Additional current or potential uses of text mining technologies include:

- Automated analysis of customer contracts for reconciling contracts with accounting policies, managing revenue recognition, controlling pricing or other contractual terms and obligations, controlling contract renewals or extensions, and assisting with any additional business insights from customer contracts
- Automated review of debt financing agreements and amendments for debt covenant management
- Automated analysis of lease agreements or other types of documents (employment agreements, employee offer letters, subcontractor

agreements, and others) for maintaining compliance with accounting standards or accounting due diligence

Tax Automation

H&R Block and KPMG are examples of tax service providers who have reported using IBM Watson for tax preparation (H&R Block, 2017; "KPMG and IBM," n.d.). At H&R Block, tax professionals have worked alongside with an IBM Watson-powered application to help clients ensure that every deduction and tax credit is found (H&R Block, 2017).

KPMG has built an application with IBM Watson to help clients secure R&D Credits. With the application, users can upload thousands of documents and analyze structured and unstructured data at rapid speeds to help identify projects that are eligible for R&D Credits, using natural language processing to understand the context (Brown & Rainey, 2018).

Another example of the adoption of machine learning-powered applications for tax preparation using structured and unstructured data is Intuit Inc. Intuit provides an application called Tax Knowledge Engine (TKE) that helps TurboTax users streamline tax preparation. The system delivers answers tailored to each tax filer by intrinsically correlating and intertwining more than 80,000 pages of US tax requirements and instructions based on an individual's unique financial situation. The system suggests what questions to ask, based on user data, and assists with computations. It includes a built-in explanation capability such that the engine can explain back the computations at any moment, for any tax concept involved (Wang, 2019).

Text mining, powered by machine learning and AI, is likely to profoundly affect tax automation. The use of these technologies will continue to progress to further automate tax preparation and tax planning tasks, with the emergence of question answering systems and potentially also virtual assistants that augment humans in addressing client-specific tax questions.

Text mining can also be used for tax audits or tax litigation analysis in taxation (income tax, sales tax, property tax, international taxation, and others). For example, text mining can analyze invoices, contracts, or other documentation for the proper tax classification of transactions or assets and taxation.

The tax authorities themselves are also expected to be significant users of these advanced technologies for tax examinations, tax fraud detection, tax avoidance or evasion, or tax policy from the perspective of governments or regulators. As an illustration, refer to the following statement from the Internal Revenue Service (IRS, n.d.):

> IRS must take full advantage of technology to improve decision-making. Modern technologies continue to change the way organizations in the private and public sectors deliver their mission, products, and services. Government executives believe digital technologies are critical to improving financial services, such as revenue collection, audits, cash management and claims management. The IRS must respond to other changes (e.g., process robotics, blockchain and artificial intelligence) and integrate technologies that enable more efficient mission delivery. For instance, the IRS has applied data and analytics to refine identity theft detection models, filters and business rule sets designed to detect refund fraud and noncompliance. By continuously monitoring their performance, the IRS has ensured a cycle of improvement in detecting and preventing identity theft. (p. 19)

Business Advisory Automation

Accountants also serve in various business advisory roles outside statutory accounting, audit, and tax. Indeed, many accountants advise or work in functions such as managerial accounting, financial planning and analysis, internal audit, compliance, forensic accounting, or information systems (IS) audit. These functions also have been significantly impacted by AI and machine learning technologies, involving data mining of both textual and non-textual data.

For example, corporate documents combined with social media and other textual data sources can be a rich source of information for assessing an organization's adherence to regulatory requirements such as privacy and security, compliance with labor laws, or compliance with industry-specific regulations (e.g., "Know Your Customer" laws in financial services).

Functions such as internal/operational audit, IS audits, or enterprise risk management require internal auditors to review copious amounts of written documentation from various sources. As Daniel Torpey, CPA, and Vincent Walden, CFE, CPA of Ernst & Young stated in their 2009 article:

> To address the full spectrum of data sources surrounding enterprise risk more efficiently, internal auditors can now incorporate unstructured data or text analytics tools into their work plans.

… Text analytics tools can be used in the context of a risk-based internal audit, as part of a forensic review of controls or business practices, or during an actual investigation (p. 42).

The authors explain that most business transactions or events are likely to have email communication associated with them. Emails contain rich metadata (information stored about the data such as origin, version, and date accessed). This metadata is a promising source of information for internal auditors.

The authors cite examples of using text analytics technologies and point out that these tools can also be used proactively within an enterprise to understand risks and identify anomalies.

They mention the example of an internal audit director at a global technology firm. This firm used text analytics tools to assess compliance risk and help prevent regulatory violations for three acquisitions in the context of a recent increase in regulatory enforcement activity associated with the US Foreign Corrupt Practices Act (FCPA).

They conclude their article by stating, "By incorporating internal audit methodologies around text analytics, auditors can also enhance their proactive risk efforts and potentially improve business performance for the clients they serve" (p. 44).

In conclusion, text mining combined with AI and machine learning approaches provides significant opportunities for automating the work of accountants and auditors to a much greater extent than it is today. Although the use of these technologies is only developing in the accounting profession, we expect that they will dramatically change the way the work of accountants and auditors is performed, including:

- More robotization of accounting tasks: meaning significant efficiency gains and more time spent on analyzing data versus collecting and recording data
- More information analyzed: meaning greater accuracy, better insights, and improved decision making; and
- More proactive and continuous monitoring of internal controls and audits: meaning more timely detection of anomalies or risks and improved business performance

References

Alarcon, J., Fine T., & Ng, C. (2019). Accounting AI and machine learning: Applications and challenges. *Accounting and Technology: PICPA's Guide to*

68   *Text Mining*

an Evolving Profession, 3–7. http://onlinedigeditions.com/publication/?m=14667&i=583202&p=0.

Blake, C. (2011). Text mining. *Annual Review of Information Science and Technology*, 45(1), 121–155. http://doi.org/10.1002/aris.2011.1440450110.

Brown, B., & Rainey, S. (2018, April 9). *Driving faster, more accurate and more beneficial tax decisions.* IBM. https://www.ibm.com/blogs/watson/2018/04/driving-faster-more-accurate-and-more-beneficial-tax-decisions/.

Chopra, S., Auli, M., & Rush, A. M. (2016, June). *Abstractive sentence summarization with attentive recurrent neural networks. Conference of the North American Chapter of the Association for Computational Linguistics: Human Language Technologies.* San Diego, California, United States. https://www.aclweb.org/anthology/N16-1012/.

Da Costa Pereira, C., & Tettamanzi, A. G. B., (2006). An ontology-based method for user model acquisition. In Z. Ma (Ed.), *Studies in fuzziness and soft computing: Soft Computing in ontologies and semantic web* (pp. 211–229). Springer.

Davis, M., Vashisth, S., Emmott, S., & Brethenoux, E. (2018, November 5). *Market guide for text analytics* (ID: G00361404). Retrieved from Gartner database.

Deloitte Harnesses the Power of Kira for Lease Accounting Contract Review. (2020, July 9). Kira systems. Retrieved July 9, 2020, from https://kirasystems.com/resources/case-studies/deloitte/.

Feldman, R., & Dagan, I. (1995). *Knowledge discovery in textual databases. The First International Conference on Knowledge Discovery and Data Mining (KDD-95).* Montreal, Quebec, Canada.

IRS, (n.d.). *Advance data and analytics.* https://www.irs.gov/about-irs/strategic-goals/advance-data-analytics.

H&R Block (2017, February 2). *H&R Block with IBM watson reinventing tax preparation.* https://www.hrblock.com/tax-center/newsroom/around-block/partnership-with-ibm-watson-reinventing-tax-prep/.

Hearst, M. A. (2003). *What is text mining?* [Unpublished Essay]. http://people.ischool.berkeley.edu/~hearst/text-mining.html.

Hearst, M. A. (2009). Information visualization for text analysis. In E. Editor (Ed.), *Search user interfaces.* Cambridge University Press. https://searchuserinterfaces.com/book/sui_ch11_text_analysis_visualization.html.

Keikha, M., Razavian, N. S., Oroumchian, F., & Razi, H. S. (2008). Document representation and quality of text: An analysis. In Berry M. W. & Castellanos M. (Eds.), *Survey of text mining II: Clustering, classification, and retrieval* (pp. 219–232). Springer.

Keim, D. A. (2002). Information visualization and visual data mining. *IEEE transactions on visualization and computer graphics*, 8(1), 1–8.

KPMG and IBM (n.d.). KPMG. Retrieved July 9, 2020, from https://home.kpmg/xx/en/home/about/alliances/ibm.html.

Kumar, B. S., and Ravi, V. (2016). A survey of the applications of text mining in the financial domain. *Knowledge-Based Systems*, 114, 128–147. https://doi.org/10.1016/j.knosys.2016.10.003.

Kumar, Y. J., Goh, O. S., Basiron, H., Choon, N. H., & Suppiah, P. C. (2016). A review on automatic text summarization approaches. *Journal of Computer Science, 12*(4), 178–190. https://doi.org/10.3844/jcssp.2016.178.190.

Lewis, C., & Young, S. (2019). Fad or future? Automated analysis of financial text and its Implications for corporate reporting. *Accounting and Business Research, 49*(5), 587–615. https://doi.org/10.1080/00014788.2019.1611730.

Nagarkar, S., & Kumbhar, R. (2015). Text mining: An analysis of research published under the Subject category 'Information Science Library Science' in Web of Science Database During 1999–2013. *Library Review, 64*(3), 248–262. https://doi-org.libproxy.temple.edu/10.1108/LR-08-2014-0091.

Nallapati, R., Zhou, B., Dos Santos, C. N., Gulcehre, C., & Xiang, B. (2016). *Abstractive text summarization using sequence-to-sequence RNNs and beyond.* The SIGNLL Conference on Computational Natural Language Learning (CoNLL). https://arxiv.org/abs/1602.06023.

Pejic-Bach, M., Krstic Z., Seljan, S. & Turulja, L. (2019). Text mining for big data analysis in financial sector: A literature review. *Sustainability, 11*(5), 1277. http://doi.org/10.3390/su11051277.

Rajman, M., & Vesely, M. (2004). From text to knowledge: Document processing and visualization: A Text Mining Approach. In S. Sirmakessis (Ed.), *Text Mining and its Applications – Results of the NEMIS Launch Conference* (pp. 7–24). Springer.

Random House Kernerman Webster (n.d.). Coreference. In *Random House Kernerman Webster's College Dictionary*. Retrieved April 25, 2020, from https://www.thefreedictionary.com/coreference.

Rush, A. M., Chopra, S., & Weston, J. (2015). *A neural attention model for abstractive sentence summarization.* Cornell University Library. https://arxiv.org/abs/1509.00685.

Sharda, R., Delen, D., & Turban, E. (2014). *Business intelligence: A managerial perspective on analytics* (3rd ed.). Pearson Prentice Hall.

Song, S., Huang, H., & Ruan, T. (2019). Abstractive text summarization using LSTM-CNN based deep learning. *Multimedia Tools and Applications, 78*, 857–875. https://doi.org/10.1007/s11042-018-5749-3.

Sparck-Jones, K. (1999). Automatic summarizing: Factors and directions. In I. Mani & M. T. Maybury (Eds.), *Advances in automated text summarization* (pp. 1–12). MIT Press. https://www.cl.cam.ac.uk/archive/ksj21/ksjdigipapers/summbook99.pdf.

Sun, T., & Vasarhelyi, M. A. (2018). Embracing textual data analytics in auditing with deep learning. *International Journal of Digital Accounting Research, 18*, 49–67. https://doi.org/10.4192/1577-8517-v18_3.

Tang, J., Hong, M., Zhang, D. L., & Li, J. (2008). Information extraction: Methodologies And applications. In H. do Prado & E. Ferneda (Eds.), *Emerging technologies of text mining: Techniques and applications* (pp. 1–33). IGI Global.

Torpey, D., & Walden, V. (2009). Accounting for words; Text analytics technology may help internal auditors uncover hidden risks and gain greater insight on business performance. *Internal Auditor*, *66*(4), 40–44.

Torres-Moreno, J. M. (2014). *Automatic Text Summarization*. John Wiley & Sons, Inc.

Tuffery, S. (2011). Text mining. In *Wiley series in computational statistics, data mining and statistics for decision making* (pp. 627–636). John Wiley & Sons, Ltd.

Verma, S., & Nidhi, V. (2019). *Extractive summarization using deep learning*. Cornell University Library. http://libproxy.temple.edu/login?url=https://search-proquest.com.libproxy.temple.edu/docview/2075709212?accountid=14270.

Wang, G. (2019, March 6). *Tech talk: Intuit's AI-powered tax knowledge engine boosts filers' confidence*. Intuit Blog. https://www.intuit.com/blog/social-responsibility/tech-talk-intuits-ai-powered-tax-knowledge-engine-boosts-filers-confidence/.

Zhang, Y., Er, M. J., & Pratama, M. (2016). *Extractive document summarization based on Convolutional neural networks*. IECON 2016–42nd Annual Conference of the IEEE Industrial ElectronicsSociety. Florence. pp. 918–922.

5 Contemporary Case Studies

To illustrate the current implementations of AI in the accounting profession, we conducted in-depth interviews with partners, principals, and AI technology leaders from the large professional services firms, including KPMG LLP, the US member firm of the KPMG network of independent member firms affiliated with KPMG International, and its global network of affiliated member firms, Ernst & Young LLP, Deloitte & Touche LLP, and Grant Thornton LLP. The interviews were semi-structured and conducted via phone conference during the first half of 2020. The length of the interviews ranged from thirty minutes to one hour, followed by correspondence via email for clarification and validation. The interviewees mentioned later in this chapter shared their perspectives, experiences, and lessons learned from AI implementations for various accounting applications.

Following these interviews, we develop and present five case studies for more in-depth analysis. The case studies include using natural language processing for risk analysis, utilizing artificial intelligence for transfer pricing services, deploying autonomous audit drones for inventory management, applying AI models to augment auditor judgment, and implementing data transformation tools and RPA to assist with monthly tax reporting needs. These case studies provide useful insights and practical guidance on how firms can leverage the power of AI to solve business problems.

Case Study #1: Use of NLP for Risk Analysis (KPMG)

Background

KPMG LLP began piloting AI in their Audit, Tax, and Advisory practices as early as 2015, according to their Global Head of Innovation, Steve Hill[1]. Hill notes, "We started an effort in collaboration with one of our strategic alliances to effectively reframe and reinvent the accounting industry using AI, cloud, and data as the three levers of transformation." Hill describes the initial goal was to use AI to supplement professional judgment to "augment the knowledge and insights of our KPMG practitioners and enhance decision-making."

Vinodh Swaminathan, Global Lead Partner and Principal with KPMG LLP's Advisory Management Consulting practice focusing on Digital Transformation, stated that KPMG successfully leveraged natural language processing (NLP) in providing Audit and Advisory risk assessment services for clients engaged in mortgage-backed securities, commercial mortgages, and other loans. Swaminathan described the following scenario: "imagine, a typical loan file for a mall in Philadelphia is probably a few gigabytes, maybe 50 different documents ranging from promissory notes to rent rolls and rental contracts with the occupants. The file has environmental surveys and engineering surveys. Think of a portfolio of documents that comprise a single loan file in which a client may be holding the loan in the portfolio to issue some sort of financial assistance to the third party." Before AI, Swaminathan explained that a KPMG professional performing this type of risk analysis would have to "literally sift through each of these 50 documents that constitute a single loan."

Today, KPMG believes that AI will eventually permeate almost every aspect of a business. On KPMG.com/us, KPMG LLP states that "AI, Automation, and Analytics are central to the success of the enterprise and will pervade critical business areas, including data, business processes, the workforce, and risk and reputation" (KPMG, n.d.).

Results

The first benefit of using NLP for this use case is that it resulted in significant efficiency gains. Swaminathan explained that "what normally took our loan professionals two weeks now can take only two hours."

A second benefit is improved quality, as KPMG loan professionals could now spend more time focusing on other areas that require judgment skills. Swaminathan remarked, "given that we reduced the two weeks down to two hours using the same staff that we have, we can start to look for risk across broader parts of the portfolio."

Finally, a third benefit of using NLP is the codification of institutional knowledge. For example, before the NLP solution was deployed, if an experienced senior manager would leave, so would their knowledge. However, with NLP, Swaminathan explained, "I have codified that institutional knowledge through these machines. I am able to, over very long periods of time, do new kinds of analytics. I have hard data now collected and codified because machines are involved over long periods of time. Again, we're able to go in and offer deep insights to clients, possibly even sometimes changing the nature of the value proposition our member firms are offering to clients."

Lessons Learned

Providing AI services involves significant investments in technology infrastructure and human capital. The focus of firms providing AI-related services should center on long-term productivity gains instead of short-term cost savings.

For KPMG firm's clients, the impact on the fee structure depends on the type of engagement and scope of services. According to Hill, "[the fee structure] varies based on the value proposition. Some of the things we're doing, some of these rates are packaged in fixed fees. We're giving our clients value back in a number of ways, either additional value in engagement or quite frankly, we get better, faster; the hours go down. It really kind of varies across the footprint."

For KPMG, Hill explained "the reality is, we're trying to extract some of the investment out of these innovations because they're difficult to build, and our intention is to evolve the economics of the business so that where we can provide efficiencies ourselves, the clients get those efficiencies quickly. We have varying kinds of pricing to help us do so." Further, Hill notes that "you can see the entire industry, especially on the advisory side, moving more toward value-based and performance-based pricing rather than just hours and rates."

Swaminathan adds that "if we view that AI projects should be done purely to recover the investment based on cost savings, a good seven out of 10 times they're probably going to fail."

Hill provides the following advice for organizations seeking to invest in AI. "The other thing a lot of people don't understand is what we call organizational capital required to make these things successful over time. You have to build this very strategically. The intelligence and the value of these appliances become greater over time, and they can be leveraged in different ways. The fungibility of this technology, when applied in patterns that can be reused – some of them proprietary to your brand, proprietary to your analytics, proprietary to your data – can be extremely powerful".

"But if you think you're going to develop a compelling investment case for the business with a return narrowed to just a single project, you are likely to be disappointed. ROI needs be appropriately and responsibly associated with the institutional knowledge, asset or component reusability, and infrastructural value that you create in the organization, again what we call organization capital, is a huge throw off of value associated with this work," said Hill.

Case Study #2: Use of AI for Tax Transfer Pricing Services (KPMG)

Background

As part of its AI strategy, KPMG Ignite is a global AI platform designed to accelerate the development of internal and client solutions focused on unstructured data (text, voice, and image) problems. It brings together KPMG professionals' in-depth domain knowledge with a toolbox of capabilities from open source, strategic technology alliances, and KPMG-developed IP. KPMG Ignite applies AI-based automation patterns to create intelligent workflows to solve business problems made complex by unstructured data. Ignite is deployed at multiple KPMG member firms to serve client bases globally. It is a containerized platform solution that provides benefits of scale and flexibility for applications supporting various business issues across multiple industries.

The KPMG Ignite platform is used by professionals of KPMG's Global Transfer Pricing Services (GTPS) practice to provide AI solutions for member firms' tax clients, specifically for transfer pricing. Transfer pricing refers to the rules and methods used to establish prices for goods and services sold between enterprises under common ownership or control. According to Komal Dhall[2], Global Leader, KPMG Global Transfer Pricing Services, one of the challenges involved in the transfer pricing process is benchmarking relevant market prices. By using AI, Dhall explained that they have successfully trained the KPMG Ignite platform to read subscription databases, analyze financial statements, and read company websites to assist with benchmarking market prices for transactions.

Results

The application of AI saves time while simultaneously increasing quality and consistency. "This type of qualitative review for humans is incredibly time-consuming and labor-intensive, but obviously the machine isn't limited in that way," said Dhall. "So what would take typically several hundreds of hours is now shortened into a simple, manageable timeframe." Consequently, tax transfer professionals "can spend time on the qualitative results and identify quality benchmarks," said Dhall.

According to Thomas Herr, Principal and National Leader, Innovation, of the Economic & Valuation Services Practice of KPMG LLP, the primary driver of AI implementation for transfer pricing is not cost savings. "The bigger benefit will be the improvements in quality and consistency," said Herr.

Herr also noted that in addition to addressing quality and consistency with transfer pricing, they want to change the nature of the process fundamentally. "Because of its manual nature, there is a well-established process in place to winnow down the amount of data that actually has to be reviewed by a human," Herr said. He added, "But it's a trade-off: in winnowing it down, you lose information, and you lose out of necessity to gain efficiency."

It is important to note that Dhall views AI as a tool to complement the work of their professionals, not as a substitute. "We're not trying to replace humans, but we're trying to enhance the quality and capability of the human in the loop in the benchmarking process," said Dhall. "The outcome is intended not only to be a more efficient process but also a higher quality analysis with more meaningful results. For example, the solution, in my view, functions as a single source of history on a many country basis, so this is the tool used globally. It's used in many countries and territories, helping to make our collective global analysis smarter."

Lessons Learned

According to Herr, one of the key lessons learned from the adoption and application of AI is good communication between subject matter experts in transfer pricing and the machine-learning specialists. "We had meetings, and things would be explained, and there was a sense that people understood it. And then we would go away and come back together again and realized we need to delve in further to gain clarity," Herr said.

This challenge was addressed by bringing the teams together more frequently. Herr describes the need "to have tighter integration with teams working much more closely together. Your subject matter experts need to work closely with the AI/ML team to ensure a good exchange of information."

Another important lesson learned was ensuring the quality of the data. "While we had a lot of data to train the models, a good chunk of that data was not of the best quality. So, we had to do quite a bit of data clean-up. And that was a larger effort than we had expected," said Herr. Also, Herr said that training KPMG professionals to properly label the data "in a way that makes it usable for machine learning" was a challenge.

Finally, Dhall recommended that companies looking to implement AI start with some well-known, repeatable processes. "We started with something manageable, doable, and something we know we can build on, because it is the backbone of many of our analyses," said Dhall. In other words, companies should be realistic and start with a relatively small-scale and straightforward project, learn from their experience developing it, and then take on more complex business problems. "From the simple use case, we're able to look across KPMG and find different applications for it" said Dhall.

Case Study #3: Autonomous Audit Drones for Inventory Management (EY)

Background

In 2017, EY[3] began using AI-enabled autonomous drones (also known as unmanned aerial vehicles or UAV) to assist with inventory counts and observations as part of its audit services. The drones use AI to navigate a site, such as a warehouse, like a human. As Sean Seymour[4], Global Mobile Technologies Leader at Ernst & Young LLP explains, "understanding which bin, which rack, which aisle to go to, all of this is based on human intelligence." By using a cloud-based asset-tracking platform, the drones perceive their surroundings, map areas, track objects through QR codes and barcodes, and provide feedback in real-time. Clients also can integrate the data captured by the drone with their warehouse management software (WMS).

Results

One of the key findings was that drones performed the same tasks as humans with 300 times the efficiency (time and costs savings) than traditional methods. The primary benefits for EY from using drone technology include faster, more comprehensive, and more accurate inventory counts, the ability for staff to spend more time on analyzing inventory risks (vs. the time spent manually capturing inventory counts in the traditional methods), and the improvement of audit quality.

Lessons Learned

One important lesson learned was the importance of having a strong network connection. As Seymour said, "whether that's Wi-Fi or whether it's a cellular connection that's built into a modem on that drone when you think about the size of some of the sites that we work on, they can be 1.5 to 2 million square feet. And inside those areas, there may be zero cellular coverage, and there may also be minimal Wi-Fi coverage as well." Seymour also mentioned that EY is exploring integrating a 5 G modem into the drone to ensure a reliable network connection. "So that then means that we can send all of the traffic directly from the drone to wherever the client wants that data to go. And not only are we going to be potentially covered from any kind of cold zones where there isn't a reception, but it also means that data analysis can be conducted in the cloud rather than on the actual physical devices that are there. And that means that they can conduct a lot more work".

Seymour cautions firms contemplating the use of drones to do their research and due diligence before adoption. As he explained, "many people still think of the drones and UAVs as toys." He pointed out that the FAA heavily regulates drones. Seymour indicated that clients sometimes do not "understand the licensing behind the scenes that are absolutely a prerequisite to using drones in the US." Violations of FAA regulations could result in substantial fines. Further, firms should be aware of the potential legal liability if a drone were to injure somebody or cause damage to property or goods.

Case Study #4: Use of AI to Augment Auditor Judgment (Deloitte)

Background

Deloitte & Touche LLP utilizes various AI technologies for risk assessment in the performance of audits. According to Brian J. Crowley[5], Audit & Assurance Senior Manager with Deloitte & Touche LLP, an objective of AI deployment is "to enhance the quality of our audits through augmenting auditor judgment by providing them with additional information relevant to a conclusion (e.g., informing an auditor of possible receivables collectability risks based on the public release of a bankruptcy filing on the internet related to an audited company's major customer)." By supplementing audit analytics with AI-enabled technologies, Deloitte & Touche LLP professionals can evaluate structured and unstructured transactional data to gain increased insights.

Results

In performing risk assessments, Crowley notes that AI models "suggest and predict correlations among datasets dynamically and tailored to those specific datasets provided, and thus suggest and predict tailored outcomes, risks, and procedures to perform in response. With these capabilities, we are pursuing more granular data at the onset of an audit as part of the planning and risk assessment processes." Crowley explains that Deloitte & Touche LLP uses optical character recognition and natural language processing to "analyze and extract insights from unstructured written language" to "identify patterns in large populations of documents such that anomalous fields or text are easily identified and summarized." Further, Crowley notes that Deloitte & Touche LLP recently "introduced additional optical character recognition functionality to process transactional evidence en masse (e.g., invoices, purchase orders, shipping documents, etc.)." Finally, Crowley describes how Deloitte & Touche LLP's 'Flux' tool "uses natural language generation AI models to analyze fluctuations in account balances over time. It provides written prose explanations to an auditor regarding the underlying component causes for those fluctuations, which allows an auditor to more easily gain an understanding of the nature of the account balance, and help to identify any risks that may be present".

Lessons Learned

According to Crowley, some of the challenges with AI implementation include "optimizing user experience and user interface, ensuring the resulting output is a high-quality audit result, and training people on how to use the tool effectively." Another challenge relates to developing AI models. "One of the greatest challenges to AI model development is data acquisition," said Crowley. "Data is required in order to train models to identify patterns that are relevant to a given business objective. More data yet is required to test those models and reach an appropriate level of confidence in real-world conditions. But not just any data will do – data format is important. Most of the data we acquire during an audit is unstructured in nature – manually-created sub-ledgers or spreadsheet analyses, contracts, transactional evidence, etc. It is extremely difficult to run these data sets through AI models at any kind of scale without some extensive pre-processing due to the variability in the format of that data."

Case Study #5: Use of Data Automation and RPA for Tax Functions (Grant Thornton)

Background

At Grant Thornton LLP, data automation is used for a variety of tax applications, such as estimating tax provisions, calculating sales tax, and reporting for state and federal income taxes, according to Christopher Spratt[6], Senior Manager of the Tax Digital Consulting practice. "We assist companies in using data transformation tools to connect directly to the data that they need to use to drive various tax functions," said Spratt.

Spratt recognizes that there are different perspectives on whether data automation and RPA constitute AI. "Perhaps it's open to interpretation as to what AI is, but I view artificial intelligence through the lens of ... automating data transformation, it's being able to drive visualization and results based off of data and leveraging of a technology or software," explained Spratt. "It's the ability to automate a process that possibly is even replacing the keystroke levels in an individual."

Spratt explained that one of the first use cases for deploying data automation was to assist a client with challenges with their monthly close. This company maintained a monthly tax provision, and they were having difficulty obtaining timely data from the accounting group to drive the tax calculations that were necessary to close out the month. Because there was not a universal chart of accounts or a companywide ERP system, "they were literally waiting on an individual in an office, in another state to be responsive and actually provide them with the financial data that they needed to start doing their tax calculations," said Spratt. "Because this company had to do some hierarchy reporting to a parent company overseas, they had a six-day close period every month. So, by the sixth business day, everything had to be recorded ... they were not receiving good information until probably sometime during day five of the close, which wasn't giving them much time."

As a result, this company had to make estimates ahead of time and then quickly adjust those estimates to ensure the proper amounts were recorded in the accounting period. "Not terrible, but not ideal by any means," said Spratt. By working collaboratively with the company's IT team, "we helped them deploy a cloud-based data transformation tool," explained Spratt.

Results

The data automation solution effectively reduced the number of days for the tax team to receive necessary information from five days to about one to two days. "We were able to work with them on the various ERP and data sources to drive a scheduled file drop starting on day one of the close," said Spratt. "And there we set it up so that there was a scheduled data drop from their ERP systems, all of the disparate systems to one location with a standardized file name and we were able to schedule that to run automatically twice a day through their ERP configurations with IT. And then, we were able to implement the cloud-based data transformation tool to look to that file destination and pull in the data every time it reran or updated. So, by doing that, we were able to pull in all the disparate data that they had. Now the tax team had access to this in day one or day two of the close."

Lessons Learned

For Spratt, obtaining valid data from the client is essential to a successful automation implementation. "I think the one lesson that I've always learned is to try and get to the source data and understand what is ultimately producing that data and what's the quickest way to get to that data," said Spratt. "And that stands true with RPA as well ... understanding specifically ... what is the keystroke level that needs to be deployed? Because if you don't get to the starting point ... the proper starting point, I think that is what can drive inefficiency, and possibly increased risk in what it is that you're looking to produce and automate."

Finally, Spratt explained the importance of firm culture and employee attitude for successful RPA implementations. "Because at the end of the day, whether it's somebody pressing start on an RPA solution or reviewing the reports that you're automating out of an analytics solution, it's really the personal experience that I think we're looking to improve. Whether it's simplifying our structure or – in most cases, it's being able to redeploy the staff to perform higher-value tasks for the organization or perform the tasks that they're more interested in spending their time on versus spending their time on mundane tasks that they may be overqualified to do based on their education and their skillset."

Conclusion

Although the specific applications of AI and RPA vary for each of these real-world use cases, there are several important takeaways. First, AI and RPA implementations change the way firms provide services to clients, adding value through efficiency gains, increased accuracy, and enhanced quality. Second, organizations must be strategic in their deployment of AI and RPA implementations by starting with processes that are manageable and well understood and then scaling up. Firms must have a good understanding of the types of projects that are best suited for automation and then obtain the necessary resources, that is, the technology infrastructure and high-quality data. Third, it is crucial to focus on the human element at the same time as technology. For example, AI implementation teams should have good communication between the subject matter experts from accounting and artificial intelligence. Firm culture and its leaders also play a role in whether AI initiatives are successful. Finally, the primary drivers of AI initiatives should focus on long-term productivity enhancements, increased quality, and accuracy, not short-term cost savings. The investments required for successful implementations of AI are substantial and require a long-term horizon and commitment by firm leadership.

Notes

1 A joint interview was conducted with Steve Hill, Principal, KPMG LLP, and Global Head of Innovation, KPMG International, and Vinodh Swaminathan, Principal, KPMG LLP, and Global Lead Partner. Steve is responsible for the lifecycle of innovation that leads to market strategies and investment prioritization. Vinodh Swaminathan is with KPMG LLP's Management Consulting practice focusing on Digital Transformation. As a leader in KPMG LLP's Management Consulting practice, Vinodh helps clients leverage intelligent automation solutions across RPA, Cognitive, and AI technologies.

   KPMG LLP is the US member firm of the KPMG network of independent member firms affiliated with KPMG International Cooperative ("KPMG International"). Some or all of the services described herein may not be permissible for KPMG audit clients and their affiliates or related entities. KPMG International provides no client services.

   KPMG International is a global network of professional services firms providing Audit, Tax and Advisory services. KPMG operates in 147 countries and territories and has more than 219,000 people working in member firms around the world. The independent member firms of the KPMG network are affiliated with KPMG International Cooperative ("KPMG International"), a Swiss entity. Each KPMG firm is a legally distinct and separate entity and describes itself as such.

2 A joint interview was conducted with Komal Dhall, Principal, of KPMG LLP, and Thomas Herr, Principal, National Leader, Innovation, EVS, KPMG LLP. Komal Dhall is also the Global Leader for KPMG Global Transfer Pricing Services. Throughout her career, Komal has focused extensively on the technology, media, and telecom industry with broad experience in complex transfer pricing analyses for companies in these sectors.

Thomas Herr is the National Leader, Innovation, for the Economic & Valuation Services practice. He has over 20 years of experience advising businesses on intragroup transfer pricing policies, transfer pricing planning opportunities, and business and intangible valuation issues.

3 EY refers to the global organization and may refer to one or more of the member firms of Ernst & Young Global Limited, each of which is a separate legal entity. Ernst & Young Global Limited, a UK company limited by guarantee, does not provide services to clients.

4 An interview was conducted with Sean Seymour, Global Mobile Technologies Leader at Ernst & Young LLP. Sean leads the EY Mobile Technologies Teams, focusing on mobilizing new and emerging technologies such as autonomous drones, mobile apps, augmented and virtual reality, AI, IoT, and cross-platform development. Since joining EY in 2014, he has continually been reinforcing and helping guide agile principles for efficient development and delivery of products.

5 Brian J. Crowley, Senior Manager of the Audit and Assurance Services practice at Deloitte & Touche LLP, contributed to a work entitled "Deloitte & Touche LLP AI Case Study" Copyright © 2020 Deloitte Development LLC.

6 An interview was conducted with Christopher J. Spratt, Senior Manager, Tax Digital Consulting at Grant Thornton LLP. In this role, he supports organizations with enhancing their tax functions through a strategic focus on people, processes, data, and technology.

Reference

KPMG. (n.d.). *Artificial intelligence: Enabling transformation.* https://advisory.kpmg.us/services/data-analytics/artificial-intelligence.html?utm_source=google&utm_medium=cpc&mid=m-00003181&utm_campaign=c-00076197&cid=c-00076197&gclid=CjwKCAjwiMj2BRBFEiwAYfTbCkQByD9lkC3bIwjjmOkfJHiXsJijKcGh-vspdVLqtrF0rYIwZ4uwCxoCL_kQAvD_BwE&gclsrc=aw.ds.

6 Challenges and Ethical Considerations of AI

From virtual assistants answering our questions to AI-powered drones and vehicles taking over tasks that humans perform, it is inevitable that AI will profoundly transform society. In the previous chapters, we have discussed many of the applications of AI and machine learning. The acceleration of AI innovation across all the accounting profession (accounting, audit, tax, and business advisory) will continue increasing at a rapid pace, and firms must be prepared to keep up.

At the same time, this transformation comes with enormous challenges. Accounting professionals need to develop controls that mitigate risks such as algorithmic bias, security, privacy, and change management. They must also rise to meet other challenges, such as the lack of standards, and the relative immaturity and lack of transparency of specific technologies.

In this chapter, we will focus on the challenges of AI for the accounting profession by discussing specifically the issues currently being debated about the risks of algorithmic bias, privacy, security, and change management. We will summarize the current state of regulations involved with the use of AI technology. We will conclude by providing an overview of AI considerations that are the most relevant to the profession and the practice of accounting in general.

Algorithmic Bias

Definition of Algorithmic Bias

Algorithmic bias is among the most notable challenges facing AI and ML systems. Several definitions of algorithmic bias exist in the literature. Among them, we like this straightforward and simple definition proposed by Gartner, in a recent research note, where the IT research firm defined it by stating that an algorithmic bias occurs when an algorithm reflects the implicit bias of the individuals who wrote it or the data that trained it (Jones, 2018).

To further increase our understanding of the algorithmic bias phenomenon, Professor Joni Jackson of Chicago State University (2018) analyzed it in more detail. He pointed out that, although algorithms are assumed to be neutral, our biases are often deeply embedded in these algorithms. For him, an important question to consider is whether the models used by the algorithms predict in a way that perpetuates existing biases. Jackson urges caution in interpreting the outcomes and the decisions that result from these models, and he suggests that, as the models become more sophisticated and learn, their predictive accuracy should continue to be tested. He also suggests bringing on diverse voices to collaborate on the design of algorithms (as people who build the algorithms are often not diverse) and to more closely examine algorithmic decisions to uncover potential adverse outcomes on specific populations due to hidden biases.

Numerous examples of algorithmic bias have been observed or identified as potential risks by researchers in recent years. Examples found in the literature include:

- Ad or search engine algorithms discriminating against specific categories of the population in terms of unfair differences in contents they see based on biased patterns or user profile characteristics,
- Recruitment systems that discriminate specific categories of applicants based on biased training data (such as data sets that lack diversity in the data),
- Facial recognition systems relying on data sets primarily composed of people with white faces that fail to recognize people with non-white faces,[1]
- Loan underwriting systems discriminating borrowers due to biased training data resulting in specific categories of borrowers experiencing lower acceptance rates or higher interest rates,
- Law enforcement systems that are making unfair crime risk predictions regarding African Americans based on biased historical data.

In the context of accounting, algorithmic bias might occur when accountants or auditors are using:

- Biased input data: such as pre-existing bias in the historical data selected for analysis, resulting in the underrepresentation of certain types of transactions due to a recent shift in the business not reflected in the chosen historical data; or
- A system that uses biased training data: for example, this would occur when the engineers who trained the system introduced a bias, intentionally or unintentionally, by missing to train the system for a particular customer segment or profile type. In such a situation, the algorithm would fail to return an accurate computation or answer by referring to a model that is not representative of the population; or
- A system that is biased in its design: such as a system that embeds biased rules or logic due to errors or omissions in the coding of the algorithm itself. Software errors (bugs) are frequent in the software development life cycle, which requires extensive quality assurance (QA) and user testing (regardless of the type of software). Unfortunately, critical software errors are sometimes only detected after the system is rolled out. That is why it is always vital for end-users to have internal controls in place to mitigate this type of risk.

Guidance for Algorithmic Bias Considerations

As software using algorithms are becoming increasingly complex, with big data analytics, AI, and machine learning, controlling for algorithmic bias has become a significant challenge. To address this challenge, the IEEE (pronounced "Eye-triple-E," which stands for the Institute of Electrical and Electronics Engineers), a significant technical professional association for the advancement of technology, recently announced a standard for algorithmic bias considerations. The standard is one of the eleven ethics-related standards currently under development as part of the IEEE Global Initiative on Ethics of Autonomous and Intelligent Systems.

According to a related working paper, the purpose of the new standard for algorithmic bias considerations is to provide software developers who create algorithmic systems with a development framework that they can use to avoid unintended, unjustified, and inappropriately differential outcomes for users. In the working paper, an unjustified bias is referred to as the differential treatment of individuals based on criteria for which no operational justification is given. An inappropriate bias is defined as a bias that is legally or morally unacceptable within the social context where the system is used (Koene et al., 2018).

Within the context of the accounting profession, we expect similar guidance to emerge from and be led by professional organizations such as the American Institute of Certified Public Accountants (AICPA), the International Federation of Accountants (IFAC), the Institute of Management Accountants (IMA), the Institute of Internal Auditors (IIA), and the Information Systems Audit and Control Association (ISACA).

Professor Lorenzo Patelli of the University of Denver (2019), a member of IMA's Committee on Ethics, calls for all management accountants to be aware that AI is not a neutral technology. AI poses challenges to their ethical professional practice based on the principles and standards of management accounting and finance. Specifically, he discusses how AI is challenging the ethical tenets of IMA's Statement of Ethical Professional Practice. In honesty, fairness, objectivity, and responsibility, he refers to the potential risks of dishonesty in the way data is analyzed in sophisticated big data analytics. Regarding the risks related to the fairness of the analysis, he stated:

> A very large data set still may not be representative of the overall phenomenon for two main reasons. First, the use of current data may not be representative of future trends. Hence, it is unfair to neglect factors that are not heavily represented currently. Second, the most dominant factors may not be the most consequential. Thus, ignoring or undervaluing historically underrepresented factors violates fairness because it may aggravate biases and cause severe unintended consequences such as discrimination. (p. 12)

Regarding objectivity and responsibility, he mentions such potential risks and challenges as the lack of flexibility to changes, inability to explain the outcomes of AI, and difficulty attributing responsibility for the results due to the complexity of AI systems and individuals and organizations struggling to accept responsibility for the consequences. He concludes that:

> Management accountants must formulate ethical principles for the design of AI algorithms, recognize ethical issues implied in the development of AI-powered software, and resolve ethical mishaps caused by the implementation of AI solutions. (p. 12)

Professional organizations have started to review their codes of ethics and standards to identify potential areas where AI ethics and bias might have to be addressed.

In 2018, the International Ethics Standards Board for Accountants (IESBA), an independent global standard-setting board (affiliated with the IFAC), formed a Technology Working Group (TWG). The purpose of the TWG is to analyze the impact of the latest trends and developments in technology on the ethical behavior of professional accountants and IESBA's existing International Code of Ethics for Professional Accountants. In the initial phase of this initiative, completed in December 2019, the TWG concluded that the Code currently provides high level, principles-based guidance for most technology-related ethics issues. However, it also identified key areas where the material in the Code could be enhanced (IESBA, 2020). Some examples of recommended enhancement areas are summarized below:

- Highlight a broader societal role for professional accountants in promoting ethical behavior as a critical, consistent foundation for organizations, particularly when developing and using technology.
- Revise the Code to deal with the threats created by the complexity of the professional environment more effectively in which professional accountants perform their professional activities.
- Revise the Professional Competence and Due Care subsection by expanding a professional accountant's responsibility to be transparent.
- Strengthen the concept of accountability outlined in the Code (by including references to technology in provisions relating to relying on the work of others).
- Revise the Confidentiality subsection considering the increased availability and use of personal and other sensitive data, to consider privacy-related matters and protect information actively.
- Strengthen the provisions relating to auditor independence (to address potential threats to independence, such as those created by the sale or licensing of technology applications to audit clients and others).

However, this effort from professional organizations remains in an early stage, and more guidance is expected in the near to medium-term future.

In practice, few organizations have an ethical framework in place to address AI and algorithmic bias risks today.

In a recent press release, Irfan Saif, a principal AI leader for the Risk & Financial Advisory practice at Deloitte & Touche LLP, stated:

For many organizations, a steep AI learning curve awaits. Traditional business professionals will need to learn how to team with data scientists and technologists to achieve strategic goals and to explain the changes in the environment. And those developing algorithms and managing data will need to be specially trained to identify and mitigate bias within AI applications. An educated and tech-savvy workforce is better positioned to ethically embrace the opportunities that AI use creates (Deloitte, 2019, para. 7).

Security, Privacy and Change Management Risks

Security and Privacy Risks

The challenges of AI are not limited to the risks of algorithmic bias. The design and deployment of AI technologies often come with increased risks in security and privacy. Today's AI systems involve complex processing of structured and unstructured data using extensive libraries of algorithms; thus, they are often interconnected with a great variety of third-party applications, systems, and devices (mobile computing, Internet-of-Things). This higher level of sophistication and interconnectivity makes them more vulnerable to potential misuse of administrative privileges, mismanaged access controls, malicious code, or attacks.

Besides, in big data, AI systems involve much more massive amounts of data than ever before. As Professor Joshua Kroll of the University of California Berkeley (2018) points out, an increasing number of business decisions are made automatically. These business decisions are driven by systems that employ machine learning, data analytics, and AI to derive decision rules using data instead of having humans code the rules. This shift to data-driven systems and software-mediated processes creates new data governance requirements for organizations.

Professor Kroll highlights, for example, that any data collected and retained pose some risk of breach or compliance issues with privacy laws or other hazards. He suggests that the data collected should be limited to only what is essential. Further, he recommends avoiding retaining data once they are no longer business-critical, secure the data at all times from outside hackers, and manage potential deliberate misuse by insiders (i.e., data should always be encrypted at rest and in transit). He also suggests that the retained data could be scrubbed and aggregated to a lower level of sensitivity. Certain categories of data could be identified, such as personally identifiable information (PII), and be treated safely. Other recommendations from Professor Kroll include:

- Form a cross-functional Data Use Review Board within the organization to approve or deny the collection of new data, investigate sensitive questions using company data, and the deployment of related insights. Beyond the risk of a data breach, the Board would assess the risks of legal noncompliance and company reputational damage because of the use of the data with the input of outside experts and panels of trusted customers.
- Review data collection and analysis practices periodically for risk assessment and provide the organization with formal social impact statements to communicate internally about the risks and the techniques or procedures to mitigate them.
- Ensure that the organization can explain what the data-driven processes are doing and how decisions are reached (such as by providing adequate explanations or documentation of these processes)
- Perform ongoing audits, including evaluating or testing systems for potential undesirable biases and designing systems that facilitate this type of review.

Change Management Risks

AI systems can be inaccurate, make mistakes, or even malfunction because of changes introduced in them or changes in their environment. Examples of change management risks include:

- A change in the application code itself:, a correction or an enhancement introduced in the application triggered an error or defect in the system.
- A change in the training data set: , a change made to the training data set resulted in defective machine learning, leading to inaccurate (or biased) results.
- A change in another system with which the AI application is interacting: that is, a change in a third-party algorithm, third-party application (e.g., enterprise resource planning, accounting), application programming interface (API), or IT infrastructure system caused an error or a malfunction in the application.

Besides, the absence of change may also be the cause of the system's deficiency: For example, an omission or a delay in updating the system or its training data set following a change in industry rules and regulations or new compliance requirements could cause severe problems. Delays would be particularly critical in the world of accounting and tax, where rules, regulations, and compliance requirements are particularly complex and change frequently.

As for security and privacy risks, because AI systems are more complex and sophisticated, and they are interacting with many other systems and devices, they are subject to increased change management risks. Increased risks represent a significant challenge for the deployment and maintenance of these systems. For example, RPA systems or bots often break due to changes in their environment (software upgrades, system integrations, compatibility with infrastructure, etc.).

To mitigate these risks, it is critical that organizations plan for adequate resources to operate, control, monitor, and maintain AI systems beyond their implementation. Failure to budget for such resources might result in the failure of the initiatives.

Regulations Related to AI

There are several federal, state, and international data privacy and security laws that currently regulate information technologies and related services. These laws apply to AI systems today, such as the Gramm-Leach-Bliley Act (GLBA), industry-specific laws such as the Health Insurance Portability and Accountability Act (HIPAA), and international laws such as the European Union's General Data Protection Regulation (GDPR). In the US, state-level privacy and security laws may require individuals and organizations to have reasonable safeguards in place to protect their customers' personal information, comply with specific breach notification requirements in case of a data breach, or take specific remediation steps based on state law. In response to the more stringent international laws (GDPR) and growing public concern, some states are advancing their regulations to protect consumer privacy and security. For example, the California Consumer Privacy Act ("CCPA") and the New York Stop Hacks and Improve Electronic Data Security Act ("SHIELD Act"), are both effective in 2020 and with application outside their respective states (Lazzarotti, 2019).

Little regulation has been written to address the risks represented using AI in the new world of hyper-automation, big data analytics, and data-driven decision systems. However, more regulation is expected in the coming years, in light of the recent scandals (e.g., Facebook with Cambridge Analytica) and the public's growing concerns related to the mass data collection and use practices of tech giants (such as Facebook, Google, and Amazon).

Among current AI-related regulation efforts, on April 10, 2019, Senators Cory Booker (D-NJ) and Ron Wyden (D-OR) proposed the Algorithmic Accountability Act of 2019, with Rep. Yvette Clarke (D-NY) sponsoring an equivalent bill in the House. The Act addresses specifically the concerns of algorithmic bias in AI systems and is the first federal legislative effort to regulate AI systems across industries in the US (Tait et al., 2019). The Act would lead to new regulations requiring individuals and organizations who use, store, or share consumer personal information to conduct periodic impact assessments on high-risk systems and their training data, and commit to addressing any identified biases or security issues in a timely manner.

Another proposed bill, introduced in the US Senate on May 21, 2019, is the Artificial Intelligence Initiative Act, which would significantly increase funding to accelerate AI research and development, education, and standards development in the US.

The need for AI regulation is also emerging as a critical global issue. For example, the Organization for Economic Cooperation and Development (OECD) issued a set of AI recommendations (OECD AI Principles) approved by OECD member countries in May 2019. In June 2019, the G20 countries adopted the G20 AI Principles drawn from the OECD AI Principles. In parallel with these efforts, there has been a proliferation of AI guidelines or principles issued by a variety of institutions and organizations, such as:

- Governments: for example, the EU (Ethics Guidelines for Trustworthy AI, by the High-Level Expert Group on Artificial Intelligence, an independent expert group that was set up by the European Commission in June 2018) and country-level initiatives (e.g., US, Canada, China, France, UK)
- Companies: for example, Google, IBM, Microsoft; and
- Industry associations and advocacy groups: for example, the Information Technology Industry Council, Partnership on AI, the IEEE (IEEE Global Initiative on Ethics of Autonomous and Intelligent Systems), Amnesty International, and Access Now (e.g., The Toronto Declaration).

The Cyberlaw Clinic of the Berkman Klein Center for Internet and Society at Harvard Law School (Harvard University) recently launched the Principled Artificial Intelligence Project to map all existing AI principles and guidelines and create a data visualization tool to summarize their assumptions, methodology, and key findings (Cyberlaw Clinic, 2019). The current dataset comprises 32 AI principles documents with their characteristics (i.e., the actor behind the document, date of publication, intended audience, geographical scope, and data on the principles themselves).

From the findings of Harvard Law School's Cyberlaw Clinic (2019), we summarize the key themes of these AI principles as follows:

- Accountability and professional responsibility
- Fairness and non-discrimination,
- Human control of technology,
- Privacy and security,
- Transparency and explainability, and
- Promotion of human values

In the following subsection, we discuss these themes in more detail and elaborate on their related ethical considerations from the perspective of accounting professionals.

Ethical Considerations

Accountability and Professional Responsibility

As Bryony Clear Hill (2020), associate manager of Ethics Awareness at the Chartered Institute of Management Accountants (CIMA), stated in a recent article, accountants possess important skills relating to ethics. They are well-positioned to take a critical role in ensuring that AI is implemented ethically in organizations. They are also committed to the ethical principles of their professional organizations' Code of Ethics.

Regarding accountability and professional responsibility, it is critical that responsibility for the decisions made or assisted by AI be clearly defined in the organization and among its service providers. This point is illustrated by the following quotation from Michael Hobbs, founder of reputable.ai, a London-based start-up, in the same article (Hill, 2020):

> The key is ensuring that decisions made algorithmically are understood up the management chain within the organization, and there is a clear line of responsibility. The company must take ownership of any decisions made by algorithms. (para. 15)

What does it mean for accountants and the Finance function of the organization in general?

Bryony Clear Hill (2020) suggested the following approach in her article:

> CFOs and senior finance managers are ultimately responsible for all finance-related decisions, including those made by AI. As such, it is key that they have a level of understanding which allows them to make informed decisions as to what AI should be used for, what data is feeding the algorithms, and how the AI is making decisions. (para. 17)

Fairness and Non-Discrimination

Accountants and auditors are involved in assessing organizational risks and compliance with laws and regulations. It is crucial to ensure that the AI systems in place do not result in unfair and unjustifiably biased outcomes or any discrimination that expose the organization to legal, reputational, and other risks. Such risks may also exist in situations where AI systems manipulate users by unfairly discriminating content based on their profile or serving hidden purposes.

Human Control of Technology

In the world of hyper-automation, users must have adequate human oversight and monitoring of AI systems. Administration includes ongoing testing of AI systems and reviewing automated outcomes to ensure that the systems work as intended and that their results are accurate and free of unjustifiable bias. Although AI may result in job losses in mundane tasks such as data entry, AP invoice processing, and reconciliations, AI will create new roles and job opportunities in analyzing AI-processed data and the design and maintenance of AI systems.

Indeed, accountants have a significant role to play. They must train and maintain the training sets of AI systems, assist with the design of AI systems that support financial reporting, tax reporting, audit, and other business processes as well as monitoring and auditing these systems and their related controls.

Privacy and Security

As discussed earlier in this chapter, privacy and security risks represent a significant area of challenges and concerns for users and providers of

AI. Standards are needed to ensure that AI systems are robust, safe, reliable and well-maintained. Also, AI systems should be frequently reviewed by both users and service providers to ensure data privacy and security risk monitoring. AI-related privacy and security, as well as issues related to human control of AI, should represent critical areas of development for accounting professionals moving forward.

Transparency and Explainability

In addition to the above considerations, data processed through AI systems should be traceable, and the outcomes should be both explainable and auditable. As Bryony Clear Hill suggested (2020), accountants should be proactive in asking questions of those designing and building AI, always ensuring that a clear understanding of inputs, decision processes, and outputs is recorded. She also added that, when running tests or trials, they should ask developers to explain the process of decision-making the algorithms are following, and that any unexplainable area should be addressed before the process goes any further.

Promotion of Human Values

Finally, the guidance on AI Principles emphasizes the need for AI systems to be human-centered, committed to the benefits of humans and society. In the context of accounting professionals, these types of ethical considerations translate into ensuring that AI systems and the outcomes derived from these systems comply with all laws and regulations, are reliable and trustworthy, and support the organization's social goals and values, including employee engagement and sustainability considerations. For example, one type of role that accountants might be involved in here would be to review an organization's internal controls over AI systems. The review would assess whether its AI systems are operating as intended and as communicated in the organization's sustainability disclosures or Environmental, Social, and Governance (ESG) reporting to investors.

In conclusion, the literature related to AI principles currently provides high-level guidelines that accounting professionals can refer to as sources of guidance and inspiration for the evolution of their codes of ethics, standards, and practices. At this stage, these AI principles represent only recommendations with no enforcement mechanisms. However, they are likely to shape the future of AI regulations and standards moving forward.

Note

1 Refer also to the recent ban by IBM, Microsoft, and Amazon of facial recognition technology used by law enforcement (Magid, 2020).

References

Cyberlaw Clinic. (2019, June 7). *Introducing the principled Artificial Intelligence Project*. https://clinic.cyber.harvard.edu/2019/06/07/introducing-the-principled-artificial-intelligence-project/.

Deloitte. (2019, October 28). *AI use expected to increase in risk and compliance efforts, but few have ethics frameworks in place*. https://www2.deloitte.com/us/en/pages/about-deloitte/articles/press-releases/ai-use-expected-to-increase-in-risk-and-compliance-efforts-but-few-have-ethics-frameworks-in-place.html.

Hill, B. C. (2020, April 6). *Building ethics into AI*. Financial Management. https://www.fm-magazine.com/news/2020/apr/building-ethics-into-ai.

IESBA. (2020, February 27). *IESBA Technology Working Group's Phase 1 Report*. https://www.ethicsboard.org/publications/iesba-technology-working-groups-phase-1-report.

Jackson, J. R. (2018). Algorithmic bias. *Journal of Leadership, Accountability and Ethics*, *15*(4), 55–65. https://doi.org/10.33423/jlae.v15i4.170.

Jones, N. (2018, September 21). *Top strategic IoT trends and technologies through 2023* (ID: G00370381). Retrieved from Gartner database.

Koene, A., Dowthwaite, L., & Seth, S. (2018). *IEEE P7003TM standard for algorithmic bias considerations. Conference Proceeding. 2018 IEEE/ACM International Workshop on Software Fairness (FairWare)*, New York, NY. https://doi.org/10.1145/3194770.3194773.

Kroll, J. A. (2018). Data science data governance [AI ethics]. *IEEE Security & Privacy*, *16*(6), 61–70. https://doi.org/10.1109/MSEC.2018.2875329.

Lazzarotti, J. J. (2019). 10 steps for tackling data privacy and security laws in 2020 for in-house counsel and HR pros. *The National Law Review*. https://www.natlawreview.com/article/10-steps-tackling-data-privacy-and-security-laws-2020-house-counsel-and-hr-pros.

Magid, L. (2020, June 12). *IBM, Microsoft And Amazon not letting police use their facial recognition technology*. Forbes. https://www.forbes.com/sites/larrymagid/2020/06/12/ibm-microsoft-and-amazon-not-letting-police-use-their-facial-recognition-technology/#d8835c718871.

Patelli, L. (2019). AI isn't neutral. *Strategic Finance*, *101*(6), 11–12.

Tait, E. J., Kantner, R. W., Galvan, H. C., & Linas J. M. (2019, June). *Proposed algorithmic accountability act targets bias in artificial intelligence*. Jones Day. https://www.jonesday.com/en/insights/2019/06/proposed-algorithmic-accountability-act.

7 Future Outlook

The proliferation of AI technologies combined with the current boom of cloud computing and the convergence of other new technologies are placing mounting pressure on the accounting profession to engage in one of the most significant transformations in its history. Some believe that AI will lead to the end of accountants. Others believe that AI will not replace accountants but augment their skills. Who is right?

In this chapter, we provide an overview of the impact of AI on the work of accountants.

We discuss the implications of adopting AI for current and future hiring of accounting professionals and new skills required to survive the upcoming transformation of the profession. From there, we examine its implications for educators and strategies to incorporate AI in the classroom to best prepare students for the new world of hyper-automation.

Finally, we conclude with our last thoughts and takeaways for the accounting profession.

Future of the Accounting Profession

Technology Changing the Landscape of the Accounting Profession

The accounting profession faces the most significant disruption of its existence since the emergence of computerized accounting in the 1960s. AI and new digital technologies (e.g., big data analytics, blockchain, internet of things, and related devices, such as sensors, drones, and virtual assistants) drive a digital revolution.

In the new digital world, business is moving smarter and faster than ever before. To stay relevant, the discipline of accounting must shift its focus from backward-looking measures of business performance to a more forward-looking approach. As we discussed in our recent article

(Alarcon & Ng, 2020), producing financial statements to becoming a strategic partner to the business represents a significant shift for the profession. The transformation includes becoming well-versed in designing and monitoring enterprise performance management (EPM) metrics and systems using the latest technology.

As we discussed in earlier chapters, several tasks traditionally performed by accountants, such as collecting, validating, reconciling, and reporting information, will become automated in the coming years with the generalization of AI and the continuous progress made with these technologies. These innovative technologies should free up considerable time for accountants and enable them to redeploy resources to accomplish this significant shift.

A similar shift is expected for auditors. In a recent white paper published by the Chartered Professional Accountants of Canada and the American Institute of Certified Public Accountants (CPA Canada & AICPA, 2020), the organizations explained that the increased adoption of AI means that auditors will spend less time gathering, correlating, formatting, and summarizing information. Instead, auditors will spend their time analyzing and evaluating the results or implications of the data. In other words, the auditor's role will move toward providing more insight. They added, "It is important to see automation, analytics, and AI for what they are: enablers, the same as computers. They will not replace the auditor; rather, they will transform the audit and the auditor's role" (p. 4).

Current research on the impact of AI on accounting jobs predicts that traditional accounting jobs will be destroyed, but new jobs will be created. Accounting systems are now able to connect directly with bank accounts and generate journal entries automatically. Manual tasks involving data entry and reconciliations, will be eliminated by leveraging AI and machine learning, combined with other technologies such as RPA. Besides, accountants and auditors currently spend a significant amount of their time collecting and reviewing information (contracts and other documents) to determine proper accounting entries or auditing accounting records. The automation of these tasks with AI-enabled RPA and document analysis tasks with text mining and natural language processing applications will enable accountants and auditors to turn to more value-added tasks.

Furthermore, as illustrated in our earlier case studies (Chapter 5), auditors will be able to increase the quality of their audits. Quality will improve with more accurate and timely results based on larger data sets and more sources of data than they were able to access and process using traditional audit methods. Additionally, auditors will perform continuous audits to streamline the audit process and provide more timely and predictive insights into the business.

Similarly, and as illustrated in our earlier case studies, AI is expected to change the role of tax accountants. AI will enable tax professionals to save time on low-value-added activities. Further, professionals can improve the quality of their services with more accurate and timelier assessments and spend more time in tax planning and advisory activities with their clients.

In addition to transforming accounting jobs as we know them, AI technologies will create new opportunities and new jobs for accountants. These include increased demand for accountants who can help design and maintain bots, algorithms, and other automation applications within the organization or service providers. The growing adoption of low-code/no-code AI platforms should also create new jobs for accountants in designing new systems in the future. Finally, as we discussed earlier, there will also be increased demand for accountants to review and audit AI systems and the internal controls around them. These system reviews will ensure compliance with accounting standards, ethics standards, laws, and regulations, including tax laws, laws related to security and privacy, industry-specific regulatory requirements, environmental laws, etc.

In summary, AI does not mean the end of accountants, but an evolution of their role. Accountants will move from being a producer of financial information to an enterprise performance advisory role, powered by AI.

As Paul Lin, Ph.D., and Tom Hazelbaker, CPA stated in their recent article (2019), "The modern technology-driven business approach drives accountants to evolve from information providers to business enhancers" (p. 51).

Firm Hiring Trends of Accounting Graduates

As pointed recently by the 2018 Rosenberg Survey (CPA Journal, 2018), technological innovations such as blockchain and artificial intelligence will dramatically transform how accounting firms are managed and staffed, and what it will mean to be a certified public accountant (CPA) moving forward.

Due to the growing demand for technology and data analytics skills, and the lack of qualified candidates among accounting graduates, public accounting firms have recently reduced their hiring of accounting graduates. Instead, firms increased the recruitment of graduates from other disciplines to fill the gaps. Choosing other fields over accounting graduates is a notable hiring trend. According to a recent AICPA report (2019a, January), hiring of new accounting graduates slowed 11% in 2018 compared to 2016 (continuing its downward trend since 2014), whereas the hiring of non-accounting graduates as a percentage of all new graduate hires was up 11 percentage points to 31%. In other words, non-accounting graduates comprised 31% of all new graduate hires in public accounting in 2018.

Commenting on these trends in a press release (AICPA, 2019b, August), Barry Melancon, CPA, CGMA, president and CEO of the American Institute of Certified Public Accountants (AICPA) stated:

> Increased demand for technology skills is shifting the accounting firm hiring model. This is leading to more non-accounting graduates being hired, particularly in the audit function.
>
> CPAs have an unmatched reputation for trust and integrity, earned through decades of working in the public interest. However, to play this vital role in the future will require an increased focus on technology. It is incumbent upon the profession to ensure accounting graduates and newly licensed CPAs have these skills and expertise needed to support the evolution of the audit. (para. 3)

Skillsets Needed in the Next Ten Years

In response to the latest trends, professional organizations in the accounting profession are actively working on increasing coverage of AI along with other technologies in their publications. They are also introducing education programs that offer their members opportunities to adapt to new technologies and embrace them in practice. However, the upskilling efforts of accountants need to go beyond acquiring knowledge about the technologies and how to use them: They must also include developing the skills they will need to assume their new roles as AI-powered accountants.

As an illustration, in their white paper on the impact of AI on the audit and the role of the auditor, CPA Canada and the AICPA (2020) discuss the changing skill sets of auditors and state:

> Advanced technologies provide a wealth of information to an auditor that enables them to make a judgment. But the auditor will still be the one making that judgment. Technology is an

enabler and is unmatched when it comes to identifying correlations among datasets or variables. However, it takes human insight and experience to ultimately understand the context underlying the output as well as the causation of the output relative to the inputs provided. (p. 10)

... As a result, it will be even more important for CPAs to have skills beyond expertise in accounting and auditing statutes to the fundamental underpinnings of accounting and auditing, and of business processes ... (p. 11)

... Audit and assurance professionals will need an increased knowledge of data science, data management and machine learning techniques (how they function, as well as their limitations). An enhanced understanding of IT, data analysis, data capture and enterprise resource planning will be needed along with skills such as critical thinking, analysis, and creativity. (p. 11)

As part of the current efforts to evolve the skillsets of the accounting profession, the AICPA and the National Association of State Boards of Accountancy (NASBA) have initiated a significant initiative (the CPA Evolution initiative) aimed at evolving CPA licensure requirements to align them with the demands of the new technology-driven business environment.

The body of knowledge required of newly licensed CPAs has grown dramatically over the years. According to the AICPA and NASBA (Tish & Reeb, 2019), there are three times as many pages in the Internal Revenue Code, four times as many accounting standards, and five times as many auditing standards today compared to 1980. The procedures historically performed by newly licensed CPAs are being automated, offshored, or delivered by paraprofessionals. As a result, freshly licensed CPAs need to know more earlier in their career and have more in-depth skills in areas such as, but not limited to:

- Critical thinking
- Professional judgment/skepticism
- Problem-solving
- Understanding of the business (including systems, controls, and risk)
- Data management and analysis
- Performance of System and Organization Controls (SOC) engagements

Consequently, NASBA and the AICPA are proposing to evolve the CPA licensure model to a "core + discipline" approach, with a more significant emphasis on technology skills. This proposed model features a substantial core knowledge test in accounting, auditing, tax, and technology that all candidates must complete and the choice of a discipline in which they must demonstrate more in-depth skills and knowledge. The proposed model recognizes the critical role played by technology in a CPA's job responsibilities moving forward by updating the core body of knowledge required for all newly licensed CPAs and allowing specialties in disciplines such as:

- Business reporting and analysis
- Tax compliance and planning, and
- Information Systems and Controls.

Accounting Educators

Strategies for Incorporating AI into the Classroom

The new CPA licensure requirements are expected to have a considerable influence on the course contents taught in accounting classes in the coming years. Some colleges have already started to incorporate data analytics in their accounting curriculum, collaborating with statistics and data science faculty or as standalone initiatives within accounting departments. For example, recent classes give students access to online resources for learning to use standard tools, such as Microsoft Excel and Access, as well as business intelligence software, such as PowerBI or Tableau, and audit software, such as ACL and IDEA, a part of their course materials and assignments.

Colleges have similarly begun to recognize the role of information technology in accounting curricula, in part due to pressures from accrediting bodies to enhance the technological content of accounting courses, including the issuance of the 2013 revised standards of The Association to Advance Collegiate Schools of Business (AACSB) requiring accredited accounting programs to incorporate technology and data analytics learning in their curriculum.

Changes in accounting programs due to advances in technology and data analytics and the challenges related to the implementation of these changes are discussed in several articles in the literature. For example, Professors J. P. Krahel of Loyola University and Miklos Vasarhelyi (2014) of Rutgers University discussed that the accounting information systems (AIS) field is undergoing extensive changes in response to emerging and rapidly changing technologies.

Professors Josette R. E. Pelzer and Roxane M. DeLaurell (2018) of College of Charleston discussed strategies to implement new AACSB requirements related to technology and data analytics in the accounting curriculum when resources are constrained, especially within the context of a teaching-focused institution.

Introducing information technology and data analytics in accounting programs is still a work-in-progress due to colleges', faculty's, and students' resource constraints. But colleges face even greater challenges now. AI and machine learning are taught in computer science or software engineering departments. Bringing AI and machine learning into the accounting classroom will require cross-departmental collaboration beyond the traditional boundaries of business schools. Universities should develop courses, projects, and case studies involving cooperation among faculty and students from departments of software engineering, data science, and accounting. In this way, accountants should be trained alongside and work closely with data scientists and AI system engineers.

Furthermore, as accountants spend more time in value-added services and business performance-enhancing activities because of AI, colleges will need to increase "soft skills" training. Development of critical thinking, problem-solving, judgment, and effective communication skills will ensure that accounting students gain an adequate understanding of business operations and organizational leadership. This will require increased collaboration and linkages among departments such as accounting, finance, MIS, and strategic management within business schools.

Adequate incentives should be implemented to foster needed cross-departmental collaboration. Faculty from non-accounting departments should be incentivized to work with accounting faculty and practitioners to help design and teach courses that are relevant for accountants. Academic career paths should offer more opportunities for faculty to teach in multiple departments. Given the social realities that academia traditionally favors professors who specialize in one discipline (e.g., computer science, data science, accounting, finance, strategic management), interdisciplinary research should be better encouraged than it is today.

In a recent article, accounting Ph.D. student C. Zhang (Rutgers University) and Professors J. Dai (Southwestern University of Finance and Economics, China) and Miklos Vasarhelyi (Rutgers University) analyzed the impact of disruptive technologies (AI, RPA, blockchain, and other emerging technologies) on accounting education (2018). The authors specifically cited the lack of qualified faculty members with a strong background in both technology and accounting as one of the biggest challenges faced by universities today.

They added: "Although basic courses, like IT and statistics, can be offered by professors in each discipline, innovative courses that bridge technology and accounting should be taught by faculty with expertise in both domains" (p. 24).

An innovative course that bridges technology and accounting would be, for example, a course that blends technology into a traditional accounting course. The authors suggest it later in their article by stating:

> Business school accounting programs are encouraged to open new courses related to IT and data analytics to diversify the course pool. Alternatively, accounting educators may also feel it useful to blend big data analytics and IT into existing traditional accounting courses such as financial accounting, managerial accounting, auditing, and taxation. (p. 26)

This line of thought is indicative of where future accounting faculty is headed and illustrates the need for accounting faculty to acquire technology skills as part of their core. The skills of accounting faculty must be like what will be expected from the accounting profession moving forward.

These skill changes do not necessarily mean that every accounting faculty needs to rewrite their course materials. Faculty should leverage existing online resources and online tutorials available on the internet (for free or for a fee) and incorporate them into their curricula. Online resources and videos may include:

- Online materials from other faculty members within the school (shared video library within the school or university),
- Online videos from online continuing education providers (e.g., Coursera, Udemy, Lynda, O'Reilly)
- Online materials from other external sources, such as other universities, professional organizations, and technology and service providers

These online resources could be leveraged to help upskill accounting faculty and incorporate these resources as part of students' assignments and exercises, case studies, and projects that would require the use of modern technologies.

Upskilling would involve a general shift of teaching methods from traditional, passive learning methods to more active learning methods. Options include experiential learning (i.e., learning-by-doing, learning from direct experience), project-based learning, and collaborative learning, where students are expected to think rather than to memorize. Considering the increased scope of learning requirements of accountants and the pace at which technologies evolve, the focus of higher education should be on teaching students how to learn rather than teaching them what to learn.

As Zhang et al. suggested in the conclusion of their article (2018): "Educators should also encourage a philosophy of lifelong learning and teach students to learn new things and adapt to the changing environment, cultivating accountants who are prepared for the future" (p. 26).

AI Training for Faculty

As discussed earlier, collaboration with computer science or software engineering departments and online resources (as mentioned in the previous section) can be used by accounting faculty to learn about new AI and machine learning technologies. Understanding how AI and ML apply to accounting is a critical part of a professional's upskilling efforts.

Also, as AI technologies increase and become more embedded in existing applications across all business areas (e.g., enterprise resource planning, accounting, data analytics), software vendors will inevitably serve as a useful source of information and training opportunities.

Beyond understanding the concepts and how they apply to accounting, faculty should also consider experimenting with some of these technologies to learn how to use them in simple exercises and projects, by working collaboratively with practitioners. Cross-training on the use of these technologies could be achieved by collaborating with adjunct and practice-oriented faculty with experience implementing these technologies in the real world.

Other suggestions include incenting some faculty members to serve as "early adopters," as suggested in Smith (2017). In this article, Professor Sean Stein Smith of Lehman College in New York City suggested:

> Ask for faculty volunteers. Have some faculty members act as "early adopters" who can then share their knowledge and

experience with the rest of the department. Seek out faculty and instructors willing to experiment and up for the challenge of learning new technology tools. Consider offering a course release or other incentive to help address time constraints. Asking for volunteers demonstrates the organization's intent toward integrating these tools and allows the most interested individuals to step forward. (para. 10)

Conclusion

As we discussed throughout this book, the role of AI in accounting is only beginning to take shape. AI applications that have emerged in the profession have been primarily focused on automating routine, mundane tasks of accountants such as data entry, reconciliations, matching, verifications, inventory counts, classification of documents, and data capture. However, the pace of technology development has increased dramatically. Moving forward, AI technologies are expected to be embedded in all core business applications. This includes integrating machine learning and deep learning capabilities, which will transform business applications from rule-based to more sophisticated, cognitive applications.

It is also expected that AI will rapidly mature, taking on not only routine, mundane tasks, but also non-routine, analytical tasks. We already see evidence of this trend in AI-enabled big data analytics and text mining applications.

Furthermore, we already see AI applied in manufacturing and supply chain (e.g., AI-enabled robots for production and inventory management) as well as other sectors such as aerospace (e.g., AI-based autopilots, drones) and transportation (e.g., driverless vehicles). Accounting and audit applications will become more autonomous over time, while still requiring human judgment and oversight by humans. In the context of accounting, this role will be filled by highly knowledgeable and tech-savvy accountants.

In this context, the accounting profession is on the verge of a profound transformation driven by the rapid deployment of AI technologies in the coming years. There will be less demand for accountants in low value-added functions (e.g., data entry, reconciliations, invoice processing, and other clerical tasks). Even in certain analytical functions, AI and automation will take over some of the tasks currently performed by accountants. However, human oversight and judgment will be required for all AI-enabled systems and processes. Also, AI will be used to handle tasks that did not exist before (such as Big Data AI analytics or continuous auditing) because, before these technologies, humans were not able to perform these tasks in an efficient way using human processing.

AI will create new challenges and new ways of doing business. As a result, the job descriptions of current accounting roles will change. New jobs will be designed to incorporate new tasks, such as ensuring the quality of data inputs into AI applications, monitoring, and controlling AI-enabled processes, reviewing outcomes from AI applications, and applying judgment to ensure accurate reporting. Accounting professionals will be accountable for managing bots, testing new algorithms as part of new implementations or maintenance, incorporating non-financial measures, predictive analytics, and business metrics as part of integrated reporting. Performing AI-based audits and continuous auditing and advising stakeholders in data-driven decisions will be a routine part of the audit and internal control functions.

In the coming decade and beyond, AI will continuously raise the bar of what it means to be an accountant. To take advantage of AI technologies in accounting and enterprise performance management, organizations will need to engage in significant training efforts to upskill their accounting teams. Their employees will be critical in the success of the implementation and monitoring of these technologies. They will also hire new talents who have the skillsets needed to thrive in the digital era.

The accounting profession has a vital role to play in leading this transformation. Accountants, auditors, and related professionals should be preparing for significant changes. They should embrace these new technologies, gain the required technical knowledge and soft skills, and develop a mindset of life-long learning to be able to adapt to the ongoing changes brought by the innovative technologies.

References

AICPA. (2019a, January 25). *2019 Trends in the supply of accounting graduates and the demand For public accounting recruits.* https://www.aicpa.org/content/dam/aicpa/interestareas/accountingeducation/newsandpublications/downloadabledocuments/2019-trends-report.pdf.

AICPA. (2019b, August 13). *Public accounting firm hiring model shifts: AICPA 'trends report'.* https://www.aicpa.org/press/pressreleases/2019/public-accounting-firm-hiring-model-shifts-aicpa-trends-report.html.

Alarcon, J., & Ng, C. (2020). The next management breakthrough: EPM, non-GAAP measures, and KPIs in a digital world. *Pennsylvania CPA Journal, 91*(1), 30–33.

CPA Canada & AICPA. (2020, June). *The data-driven audit: How automation and AI are changing the audit and the role of the auditor*. AICPA. https://www.aicpa.org/content/dam/aicpa/interestareas/frc/assuranceadvisoryservices/downloadabledocuments/the-data-driven-audit.pdf.

CPA Journal. (2018). The state of the profession: Analyzing the results of the 2018 practice management survey. *The CPA Journal, 88*(12), 26–33.

Krahel, J. P., & Vasarhelyi, M. A. (2014). AIS as a facilitator of accounting change: Technology, practice, and education. *Journal of Information Systems, 28*(2), 1–15. https://doi.org/10.2308/isys-10412.

Lin, P. & Hazelbaker, T. (2019). Meeting the challenge of artificial intelligence: What CPAs need to know. *The CPA Journal, 89*(6), 48–52.

Pelzer, J. & DeLaurell, R. (2018). Implementation of AACSB standard A7: A strategy for limited resources. *The Accounting Educators' Journal, 28*, 117–138.

Smith, S. S. (2017). Integrating blockchain and artificial intelligence into the accounting curriculum. *Journal of Accountancy*. https://www.journalofaccountancy.com/newsletters/extra-credit/blockchain-artificial-intelligence-accounting-curriculum.html.

Tish, L. J., & Reeb, W. L. (2019, November). *CPA evolution [Slide Presentation]*. NASBA. https://nasba.org/app/uploads/2019/11/CPA-Evolution.pdf.

Zhang, C., Dai, J., & Vasarhelyi, M. A. (2018). The impact of disruptive technologies on accounting and auditing education. *The CPA Journal, 88*(9), 20–26.

Glossary of Terms

Abstractive summaries: A type of automatic text summarization where the selected document sentences are combined coherently and compressed to exclude unimportant sections of the sentences.

Algorithms: A set of detailed instructions employed by rules-based expert systems.

Anaphora resolution: A semantic analysis tool which assists in resolving what pronouns (e.g., they, he, she, it) or noun phrases refer to in a text.

Application programming interface (API): A set of functions or rules that facilitates communication between applications, databases, and devices.

Artificial general intelligence (AGI): A type of AI that can perform all the cognitive tasks of the human brain. Also known as strong or broad AI.

Artificial intelligence (AI): A computer program or software application that can imitate or simulate human behavior.

Artificial narrow intelligence (ANI): A type of AI that focuses on a specific task, such as speech recognition, computers that can play chess, or self-driving vehicles. Also known as weak AI.

Artificial neural networks (ANNs): A collection of artificial neurons (also known as units) that receive data as an input, and then logic is applied to produce an output.

Classification-based systems: Systems that cast information extraction as a classification task (i.e., extraction rules are built based on a classification model).

Convolutional neural network (CNN): A type of deep neural network initially used for computer vision tasks and more recently used for natural language processing tasks as well.

Convolutional neural network (CNN) model: A framework learns sentence features and performs sentence ranking jointly, using a regression process for sentence ranking and pre-trained word vectors,

Co-reference: A semantic analysis tool that assists in finding expressions that refer to the same entity.

Data cleaning: Tools that are used in text mining to remove noise from the textual data such as spelling errors, inconsistencies, and unnecessary items and identify metalinguistic information in texts.

Data mining: A process of analyzing large data sets (i.e., "big data") to discover previously unknown patterns or relationships.

Data selection and filtering: Text mining techniques and algorithms that are used to reduce the contents to the most relevant items for the purpose of analysis or action.

Deep learning (DL): A subset of machine learning that uses artificial neural networks to discover patterns from data.

Dictionary-based systems: Types of rule learning-based system that first constructs a pattern (template) dictionary, and then use the dictionary to extract the needed information from text.

Document classification: A machine learning technique that assigns predefined classes to documents.

Document clustering: A machine learning technique that groups documents into clusters based on their similarity.

Document preprocessing: A text mining technique that includes the following subcategories: data selection and filtering, data cleaning, document representation, morphological normalization and parsing, and semantic analysis.

Document representation: Text mining algorithms that are used to transform the unstructured text into a representation that the system can interpret for the purpose of analysis or visualization.

Entity extraction algorithms: Algorithms used to extract entities such as person names, organization names, locations, dates, phone numbers, reference numbers, prices, amounts, and related items.

Expert systems (ES): Computer systems that store knowledge from human experts to emulate human decision-making.

Extractive summaries: (or extracts) A type of automatic text summarization produced by identifying important sentences that are directly selected from the document. Important sentences can be automatically determined using criteria such as word frequency, sentence position, presence of title word, or other criteria, and using a training model (machine learning approach).

Graphical user interface (GUI): The tool through which RPA robots replicate human activity by observing the user complete a task. In other words, a script is generated through a screen recording of mouse and keyboard actions while completing a task.

Hyperautomation: Refers to the combination of RPA tools and machine learning applications.

Intelligent information extraction: Information extraction using machine learning approaches.

Information extraction (IE) algorithms: Algorithms that use various machine learning approaches, including rule learning-based methods, classification-based methods, and sequential labeling-based methods.

Latent Dirichlet allocation (LDA): A type of semantic model and algorithm which refers to techniques and systems that identify topics from the words of a collection of documents.

Latent semantic analysis (LSA): A type of semantic model and algorithm which refers to techniques and algorithms that assist in uncovering synonyms, homonyms, and term dependencies (such as pairs or groups of words).

Machine learning (ML): A subset of AI that uses algorithms to analyze data, carry out specific tasks, such as making predictions, and does not rely on explicit instructions provided in a rules-based system such as in Machine Reasoning (MR) systems.

Machine reasoning (MR): The ability of a computer to draw conclusions from a knowledge base using automated inference techniques that can imitate or simulate human inference, such as deduction and induction.

Mining: A text mining technique that includes clustering, classification, entity, and relation extraction.

Morphological normalization: Refers to natural language tasks such as stemming, lemmatization (i.e., reduction of words to their stems), and part-of-speech tagging.

Named entry recognition (NER): A type of algorithm that identifies relevant nouns of named entities such as people, places, organizations, or dates.

Natural language generation (NLG): Enables computers to produce human language so that people can understand computers.

Natural language processing (NLP): A subfield of AI that focuses on the interaction of computers and people using human languages.

Natural language understanding (NLU): Enables computers to understand instructions provided in human language.

Parsing: Refers to assigning syntactic structure to the normalized text, including text segmentation, sentence chunking into smaller syntactic units such as phrases, and the identification of syntactic relations between the identified units.

Part-of-speech (POS) tagging: A type of algorithm that assigns to each word an identifier, such as noun, verb, adjective, and others.

Reinforcement learning: A process in which a computer algorithm trains itself, learning from data through trial and error.

Relation extraction: Algorithms used to identify and characterize relations between entities such as person-organization (e.g., an employee of), person-location (e.g., born in), or organization-location (e.g., headquartered in).

Robotic process automation (RPA): A software application (robot or bot) that automates a business process by replicating the actions of humans performing tasks within digital systems, such as manipulating or transferring data.

Rule-based systems: Types of rule learning-based systems that use general rules instead of a dictionary to extract information from text.

Rule learning-based systems: Systems that use predefined instructions on how to extract the desired information (i.e., words or text fragments) from the text.

Semantic analysis: Tools that further increase the system's ability to interpret the meaning of texts, by resolving semantic ambiguities using techniques such as word sense disambiguation, anaphora resolution, and co-reference resolution, and by assessing topical proximity among and within the documents.

Semi-supervised learning: A hybrid of supervised and unsupervised learning using both labeled and unlabeled data during the training process.

Sequential labeling-based extraction systems: Systems that cast information extraction as a task of sequential labeling. In sequential labeling, a document is viewed as a sequence of tokens (i.e., words), and a sequence of labels (such as part-of-speech tags).

Supervised learning: A process in which a computer algorithm learned from a set of training data that is labeled (tagged with certain attributes such as poor credit or good credit) and paired as input and output variables (X results in Y).

Tensor processing unit (TPU): An application-specific circuit developed by Google and used to increase processing speeds for machine learning and deep learning applications.

Text mining: A process of extracting information from various text sources (such as Word documents, PDF files, social media posts, emails, websites, articles, XML files, and others) to discover patterns, trends, and themes.

Text summarization: Consists of a reductive transformation of a source text to summary text through content reduction by selection and generalization on what is important in the source.

Unsupervised learning: A process in which the computer algorithm only learns from unlabeled input data (i.e., the outputs are unknown).

Visualization: A text mining technique that includes visualization techniques for multidimensional data and text summarization.

Visualization techniques: Graphical representations (of the data mined from texts) such as word clouds, tag clouds, histograms, scatter plots, line plots, box plots, network graphs, and other graphs commonly used for representing text mining analysis results (such as clustering, topical proximity analysis, sentiment analysis or other analyses).

Word sense disambiguation (WSD): A semantic analysis tool that enables systems to interpret words that have multiple meanings (i.e., word senses), depending on the context.

Wrapper systems: A wrapper is an extraction procedure, which consists of a set of extraction rules and program codes to extract information from certain structured and semi-structured documents such as Web pages.

Index